TABLE OF CONTENTS

Alaska Lights

Do you like sunshine? All day long? If so, then you would like Fairbanks, Alaska, in June. The sun shines for almost 24 hours on June 21. The sun rises around 2:00 in the morning. It sets around midnight. And the two hours in between are not very dark.

Six months later, the opposite happens. The day is dark for about 21 hours. Sometimes the northern lights appear. Many colors dance across the sky. They look like waves.

Fairbanks is one cool place to be, in summer or in winter!

Read the diary below.
Fill in the blanks with a correct word from the word box.

June 21, 1956

It is the ___longest___ day of the year. The sun

___rose___ at two o'clock in the morning. I was still tired!

But the sunshine made it hard to go to ___bed___ .

Tonight the sun will set at _____ . It will be night

for only _____ hours. A very long day!

December 21, 1956

Today is the _____ day of the year. It will be

_____ almost all day long. But maybe the beautiful

northern _____ will appear. I love the

_____ season in Alaska!

WORD Box ▶ ▶ ▶ ▶

dark	midnight	sleep
lights	rose	two
longest	shortest	winter

Day or Night?

You are visiting Fairbanks, Alaska, at the end of **June.** Color the sun or the moon to tell what you would see at each of the times given.

8:00 a.m.

10:00 p.m.

4:00 a.m.

1:00 a.m.

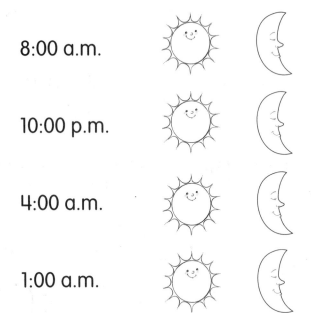

You are visiting Fairbanks, Alaska, around **Christmas.** Color the sun or the moon to tell what you would see at each of the times given.

9:00 a.m.

12:00 noon

1:00 p.m.

4:00 p.m.

Northern Lights

Look at this winter scene.
The northern lights are out!
Use the color guide to color the northern lights.

Color Key

1 = orange   **3** = violet   **5** = red   **7** = blue

2 = pink   **4** = green   **6** = black   **8** = yellow

• EMC 6305 • U.S. Facts & Fun

George Washington's
WOODEN TEETH

Wooden teeth? Did our first president have a mouth full of wood? People have told this tale for a long time. But it is not true.

George Washington had false teeth. George had two sets of dentures, but they were not wooden. His false teeth were made of many things. There was gold, lead, cow's teeth, human teeth, and hippopotamus ivory. Springs held the top teeth to the bottom teeth. George had to bite down hard to keep his mouth from flying open. It's no wonder he's not smiling on the dollar bill. Say "cheese," George!

U.S. Facts & Fun • EMC 6305 • ©2005 by Evan-Moor Corp.

Read the sentences.
Each sentence goes with an object.
Draw a line to the correct object.

1   Washington's teeth were not made of _____.

2   Some of his teeth came from a _____.

3   A _____ held his top teeth to his bottom teeth.

4   Washington's face is on a _____.

BRUSH YOUR TEETH, GEORGE!

Help George find his toothbrush!
Can you find 10 toothbrushes in this picture?
Circle each one.

Look at each picture below.
Color the picture if it is good for your teeth.

GEORGE'S DOLLARS

Look at the dollar bills in each column.
Find the ones that match.
Draw a line to connect them.

Design your own George Washington dollar.
Draw and color it any way you'd like.

See You Later, Alligator!

It looks like a log. Then it sinks below the water. See you later, alligator!

Alligators live in two places. They live in China and in the southern U.S. They like warm places. All alligators are coldblooded. Hot weather makes their temperature go up. They need to be warm to digest food.

Alligators live in warm mud during the winter. In spring, female alligators lay eggs in a mud nest. Baby alligators break out of their shells. They race into the water to find food. See you later, baby gator!

I KNOW THIS!

Read each sentence.
Write **T** if it is true.
Write **F** if it is false.
Then cross out the "false" word.
Write the word that makes it true.

Words taste yummy!

T or F   **Word**

_____   1. Alligators are warmblooded.   _____

_____   2. Baby alligators hatch from eggs.   _____

_____   3. Alligators live in the northern U.S.   _____

_____   4. In winter, alligators live
                in warm mud.   _____

_____   5. Hot weather makes their
                temperature go down.   _____

_____   6. Alligator eggs are laid in
                a grass nest.   _____

_____   7. There are alligators in China.   _____

Go, Baby Gator!

This baby alligator is lost.
Help him find his way to the water.
Don't let him go near the big hungry alligators!
They eat little gators for breakfast!

HELP ME, PLEASE!

HOME SWEET HOME

Ten Little Gators

The word **ALLIGATOR** appears ten times in this word search.
Look across, up and down, and backward.
Circle each word.
Cross off an alligator below when you find each one.

```
R  B  R  O  T  A  G  I  L  L  A
O  A  L  L  I  G  A  T  O  R  L
T  L  F  P  J  U  I  E  L  Y  L
A  L  L  I  G  A  T  O  R  B  I
G  I  C  T  D  W  M  X  O  R  G
I  G  R  O  T  A  G  I  L  L  A
L  A  L  L  I  G  A  T  O  R  T
L  T  K  C  N  H  Q  Z  V  G  O
A  O  A  L  L  I  G  A  T  O  R
S  R  O  T  A  G  I  L  L  A  D
```

GO FOR THE GOLD!
THE CALIFORNIA GOLD RUSH

"It's gold!" That's what James Marshall thought when he saw gold in the American River. The California Gold Rush had begun! The year was 1848.

Gold was found in rivers. Miners shook pans of water and dirt until nuggets appeared. Gold was found in rocks, too. Miners worked hard to dig out the pieces. The biggest piece found in California was 195 pounds!

People came from all over the world. They wanted to get rich. Some found gold. Many did not. But California grew and grew. Today it is called the Golden State. Now you know why!

Read each sentence.
Unscramble the bold word or number.
Write the word on the line.

1. James Marshall found **logd** at Sutter's Mill. _____

2. The Gold Rush started in **8418**. _____

3. Gold was in rivers and **csrok**. _____

4. The biggest piece was **915** pounds. _____

5. Now California is called the **IdonGe** State. _____

6. A lump of gold is called a **gungte**. _____

STRIKE IT RICH HERE!

RHYME TIME!

Read each riddle.
The two words in each answer will rhyme.

What is green and grows on nuggets?

_____old   _____old

Where do gold diggers eat?

At the _____iner _____iner

Where do you dig for evergreen trees?

At a _____ine _____ine

WHERE'S THE GOLD?

Something is hidden in this puzzle.
You can "mine" it by coloring the pieces.

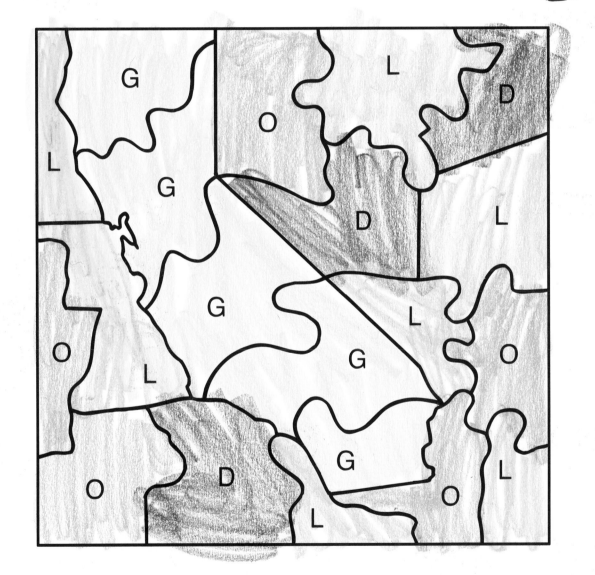

The hidden "gold" is the shape of _____ !

Frontier Fun

If your friend started acting like a dog, what would you think? Could you say, "Poor doggie, poor doggie, poor doggie," and not laugh? Pioneer kids could. They turned this silly stuff into a fun game.

Life out on the prairie was lonely. Kids had to think up games to play. They ran races, played leapfrog, and threw horseshoes. Hide-and-seek was hard because there were almost no trees!

Most of their toys were small and homemade. They had marbles made of dried clay. Some games used buttons. Dolls were made of corn husks, fabric, and sticks. After their chores were done, pioneer kids knew how to have fun!

Read each sentence.
Choose the word or words that make the sentence true.
Write the word on the line.

1. Life on the prairie was _____ .

   crowded   lonely   easy

2. Pioneer kids had to think up their own _____ .

   chores   names   games

3. It was hard to play hide-and-seek because there were few

   _____ .

   buffalo   children   trees

4. Marbles sometimes were made of _____ .

   dried clay   sticks   cowhide

5. Dolls sometimes were made of _____ .

   plastic   corn husks   shoes

Micah's Marbles

Micah and Sarah are playing marbles.
Color Micah's large marbles yellow.
Color Sarah's small marbles brown.
Connect the numbers on Micah's
marbles to see who won the game.

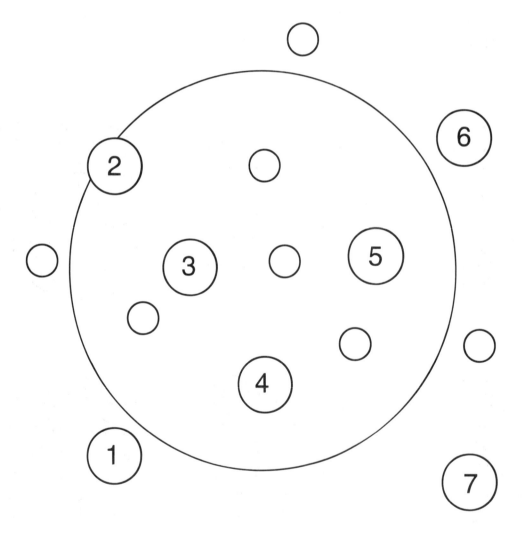

_____ won the game.

U.S. Facts & Fun • EMC 6305 • ©2005 by Evan-Moor Corp.

BUTTON TICK TACK TOE

Here are six tick tack toe games.

In each square is a button.

Make an **X** on the button if it has two holes.

Make an **O** on the button if it has four holes.

Draw a line through the winning row for each game.

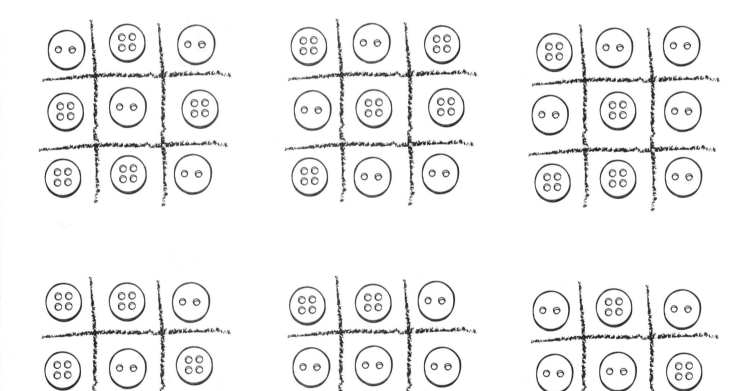

Apple Tree Man

Crunch! Yum! Nothing beats a good apple for a snack. Apples come from trees. And apple trees come from seeds. But where did all the seeds come from? Most of the apple trees in Ohio, Indiana, Illinois, and Michigan came from one place—the Apple Tree Man.

Johnny Chapman was a good tree farmer. In the 1800s, he carried a bag of apple seeds on his back as he traveled. When he found a good place, he cleared the land. Then he planted apple orchards.

He lived alone and was a poor man. His clothes were too big. He liked to go barefoot. People thought he looked funny. But they loved this man they called "Johnny Appleseed."

U.S. Facts & Fun • EMC 6305 • ©2005 by Evan-Moor Corp.

Read each sentence.
Color the apple **green** if the sentence is true.
Color the apple **red** if the sentence is false.

1 Apples grow on bushes.

2 Johnny Chapman planted apple seeds.

3 His nickname was Johnny Appletree.

4 He traveled into Ohio and Indiana.

5 Chapman was a rich man who loved apple trees.

Apple Parts

Look at the big apple.
Label the parts.
Use the words in the word box to help you.
Color it like your favorite kind of apple.

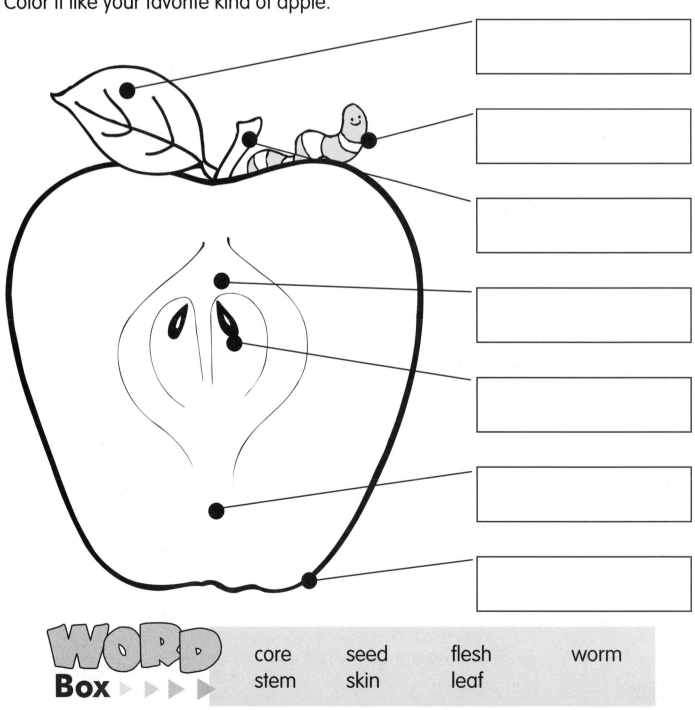

WORD Box ▶ ▶ ▶ ▶ ▶

core   seed   flesh   worm
stem   skin   leaf

An Apple a Day

Read each riddle.
Find the answer for each one.
Draw a line from the riddle to its answer.

 1. How can you tell when an apple is sunburned?

 2. Why was the apple all alone?

 3. What do you call an apple that gets run over by a truck?

 4. What do you call a giant with apples in his ears?

 5. What did the apple say to the hungry bully?

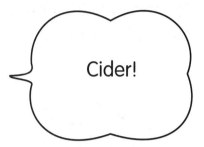 Cider!

 Don't pick on me!

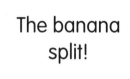 The banana split!

 Anything you want! He can't hear you!

Its skin turns red!

Cow Catchers

Cows can't hide very well. But they can still be hard to catch. Just ask the cowboys from the 1870s.

Cowboys had a hard job. They had to get a bunch of longhorns from Texas to Kansas. These beefy cows were tough, big, and fast! Cowboys rode horses to "round up" a herd. The cowboys made the cows run and run. Soon, the cows were too tired to run away. Then the cowboys could steer the longhorns along the trail.

The "Long Drive" lasted about four months. Cowboys lived outdoors with the snakes, bugs, and open sky. It was a hard life. The cowboys' job ended when the railroad was built. Then cows were shipped by train. The Long Drive was over.

U.S. Facts & Fun • EMC 6305 • ©2005 by Evan-Moor Corp.

Read each sentence.
Find the word that is wrong.
Circle it.
Write the opposite to make it correct.

1. Cows can hide very well. _____

2. A cowboy's job was easy. _____

3. Longhorns were big, tough, and slow. _____

4. Cowboys made the cows rest and rest. _____

5. Cowboys lived indoors. _____

6. Railroads helped start the Long Drive. _____

Long Drive Challenge

Not all longhorns made it to Kansas. Some ran off. Some died along the way. Help these cows get from Texas to Kansas. They cross paths along the way. Color the cow that gets lost.

Word Roundup!

Some "cowboy" words are hiding.
Look in the word search for the word box words.
Circle each one.
Look up and down and across.

```
R  I  R  B  E  E  F  Z  Q  C
O  S  D  Y  T  F  P  K  B  L
U  T  E  X  A  S  C  R  K  O
N  R  C  E  J  B  O  A  O  N
D  A  U  G  B  X  W  I  K  G
U  I  V  H  U  I  B  L  A  D
P  L  O  N  G  H  O  R  N  R
E  D  A  L  S  E  Y  O  S  I
J  S  T  E  E  R  H  A  A  V
M  A  G  W  N  D  F  D  S  E
```

Box ▶ ▶ ▶ ▶

longhorn	beef	long drive	cowboy
Kansas	roundup	bugs	trail
Texas	steer	railroad	herd

Mighty Big Trees

Look up! Way up! Way, way up! Can you see the top of the tree? If it's a redwood, you probably can't. The tallest tree in the world is the California redwood. It can grow to 360 feet tall. That is taller than the Statue of Liberty! It is the state tree of California.

The redwood's wood is red. It has needles and cones like a Christmas tree. Redwoods grow on the coast of California. Some are 1,000 years old. One redwood in California is 2,200 years old. That would be a lot of birthday candles!

U.S. Facts & Fun • EMC 6305 • ©2005 by Evan-Moor Corp.

I KNOW THIS!

Read each sentence.
Choose the word or words that make the sentence true.
Write the word(s) on the line.

1 The redwood is the state tree of _____ .

   Texas   Florida   California

2 They can grow to be _____ feet tall.

   360   1,000   2,200

3 The Statue of Liberty is _____ some
   redwoods.

   taller than   shorter than   the same size as

4 The redwood has _____ .

   needles   cones   needles and cones

5 Many redwoods live more than _____ years.

   360   1,000   5,000

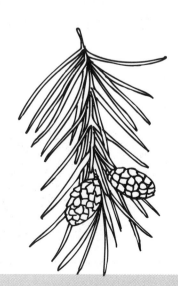

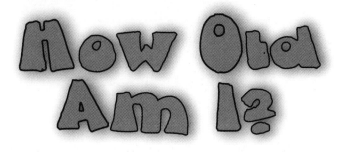

How Old Am I?

Trees tell their age.
Each ring is a year.
Count the rings inside each tree.
Do <u>not</u> count the bark (the outside).
Write the age of the tree on the line.

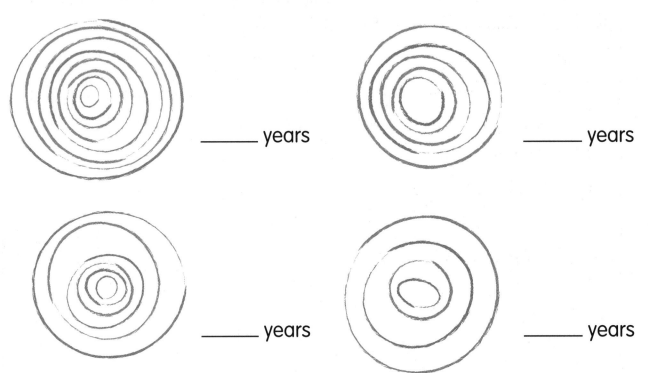

_____ years

_____ years

_____ years

_____ years

Decorate this birthday cake for the youngest tree.
Draw the correct number of candles on the cake.

fine forest friends

Lots of animals live in the forest. There are 10 hiding in the redwood trees.

Find each of the animals. Color each animal.

Run, Bird, Run!

Faster than a rattlesnake! Quicker than a lizard! It's a bird. It's a . . . roadrunner!

This speedy bird can run up to 15 miles per hour. It can fly if it wants to, but running is more useful. The roadrunner can even jump straight up to catch a meal. It eats bugs and desert animals like snakes and mice.

Most birds are afraid of humans. But the roadrunner is not scared of people. It might walk right up to get a close look at someone. Then off it goes again!

U.S. Facts & Fun • EMC 6305 • ©2005 by Evan-Moor Corp.

Read each sentence below.
Circle **yes** or **no**.

1 A roadrunner can run 15 miles per hour.   yes   no

2 Roadrunners are afraid of people.   yes   no

3 Roadrunners cannot fly.   yes   no

4 A roadrunner can catch a snake.   yes   no

5 Roadrunners can jump straight up.   yes   no

Think Fast!

Use the letters in **DESERT ROADRUNNER** to make lots of words.
Write them on the lines below.

DESERT ROADRUNNER

red

toad

Sun

U.S. Facts & Fun • EMC 6305 • ©2005 by Evan-Moor Corp.

Picture Words

Look at each pair of pictures.
Together, they make a new word.
Find that word in the box.
Write it on the line.

_____

_____

_____

_____

_____

_____

WORD Box ▶ ▶ ▶ ▶

anthill	cowboy	eggshell
rattlesnake	roadrunner	butterfly

Sweet Trees

It pours on pancakes. It warms your waffles. Maple syrup is a sweet breakfast treat! And it all starts with a bunch of trees.

Maple syrup comes from sugar maple trees. Each tree is "tapped" in the spring. To tap a tree, a farmer makes a hole in the tree about three inches deep. A spout is put in the hole. The sap of the tree runs out of the spout into a bucket. One tree will give about ten gallons of sap each year. That will make one quart of syrup.

A tree must be about 40 years old before it can be tapped. It must be strong and healthy. Tapping does not hurt the tree. A good tree can give sap for more than 100 years. That is a very sweet tree!

Read each question.
Find the correct number on a maple leaf.
Write it on the line.

1 How many inches deep is a tap? _____

2 About how many gallons of sap can
a tree give each year? _____

3 How many years old should a tree be
before it is tapped? _____

4 For how many years could a tree give sap? _____

5 **BONUS!** How many gallons of sap could
a tree give in its lifetime? _____

40   1,000   3   100   10

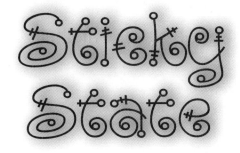

One state in the U.S. makes more maple syrup than any other. Do you know which one it is? Color the picture below to find out.
Use the colors found in fall maple leaves.

Color Key

B = brown   **Y** = yellow   **R** = red   **O** = orange   **G** = green

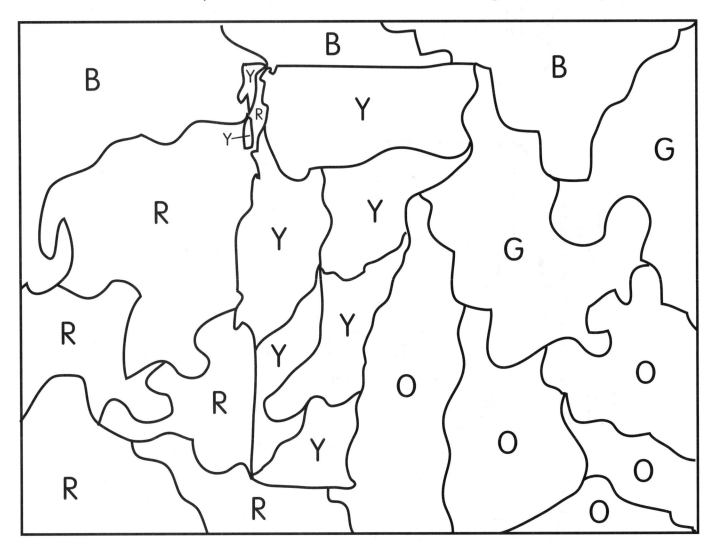

Fill in the two missing vowels to name the state.

V ___ R M ___ N T

U.S. Facts & Fun • EMC 6305 • ©2005 by Evan-Moor Corp.

Fill in the empty waffle squares. All but one of the words is from the story.
The squares will solve this riddle:

Where did the baker find his missing lid?

In the _____ .

A Turkey or an Eagle?

How do you pick a national bird? Should it be big and gentle? Should it be strong and beautiful? Some of America's first leaders wanted the bald eagle. But Benjamin Franklin said, "No way!" He had another bird in mind. He wanted the wild turkey.

The turkey is a large bird. It eats seeds and insects. The turkey was important at the first Thanksgiving!

But some thought the turkey was a poor symbol. It was not strong and beautiful. The eagle was a better choice. To Native Americans, an eagle feather was a sign of bravery.

Today, our national bird, the bald eagle, stands for peace and strength.

U.S. Facts & Fun • EMC 6305 • ©2005 by Evan-Moor Corp.

I KNOW THIS!

Read each sentence.
Does it tell about a turkey or an eagle?
Circle the turkey or eagle to show your answer.

 Turkey here! Nice to meet you.

  How do you do; I am an eagle.

1. Ben Franklin liked me best.

2. I like to eat seeds and bugs.

3. My feathers stand for bravery.

4. I was at the first Thanksgiving.

5. I am America's national bird.

6. I stand for peace and strength.

Wacky Birds!

Look at the picture below.
What is wrong with these birds?
Fill in the blanks.

Turkeys...

can't hang _____ .

don't _____ .

don't _____ takeout.

don't wear _____ .

don't _____ newspapers.

Eagles...

aren't _____ of _____ .

don't have _____ like toucans.

don't have _____ like peacocks.

don't eat _____ .

don't wear _____ .

U.S. Facts & Fun • EMC 6305 • ©2005 by Evan-Moor Corp.

State Bird
— Words —

Each state in the U.S. has a state bird. Unscramble the bird word beside each state name. That's the state bird!

1. Minnesota   **onlo**   _____

2. Utah   **sae lugl**   _____

3. Louisiana   **cpeinla**   _____

4. New Hampshire   **leuprp nhfic**   _____

5. Arizona   **sucatc nwer**   _____

6. Connecticut, Michigan,
   and Wisconsin   **inorb**   _____

7. All of these states have
   this as their state bird:

   Illinois, Indiana,
   Kentucky, North Carolina,
   Ohio, Virginia, and
   West Virginia.   **niraldca**   _____

WORD
Box ▶ ▶ ▶ ▶

cardinal	loon	pelican	seagull
purple finch	cactus wren	robin	

Name That FLAG!

Did you know that the U.S. flag has two names? It is called "Stars and Stripes." It is also called "Old Glory." No matter what you call it, the flag stands for America.

The stars and stripes tell about our country. There are 50 white stars on the flag. Each star stands for a state. There are 13 stripes, 7 red and 6 white. They stand for the first 13 states.

Each color on the flag has a meaning, too. The color red stands for courage. White is for purity, or standing up for what is good. Blue stands for friendship, loyalty, truth, and honor.

Yes, our flag tells all about America!

I KNOW THIS!

Read each clue.
Write the answer in the puzzle.

Across
1. There are 50 _____ on the flag.
3. The color _____ stands for purity.
5. One name for the flag is "Old _____ ."
6. Each star stands for a _____ .

Down
1. There are 13 _____ on the flag.
2. The color _____ stands for courage.
4. The color _____ stands for loyalty and friendship.

©2005 by Evan-Moor Corp. • EMC 6305 • U.S. Facts & Fun

How many STARS?

Count the stars on the United States flag.
Fill in your answers in the box below.
Color the flag.

There are _____ stars.

I see _____ rows with 6 ☆'s.

I see _____ rows with 5 ☆'s.

Make Your FLAG

A flag stands for a country or a state.
Some flags stand for a person or an idea.
If you had a flag that shows something about you, what would it look like?
Draw your flag below.

A Dollar or a Buck?

"That bike costs big bucks!" Do you know what that means? The word **buck** means "a dollar." In frontier times, a hunter got one dollar for the skin of a buck, a male deer. Today, we still use the word **buck** to talk about money.

For a long time, each state in the U.S. had its own money. That was a big problem. Today, money across the U.S. is the same.

Both coins and paper money are called **currency**. Coins are made of metal. Coins are made at a place called a **mint**. There are four mints that make coins. Paper money is made at two places in the United States. Pennies or dollars—it's still money. And it can add up to big bucks!

U.S. Facts & Fun • EMC 6305 • ©2005 by Evan-Moor Corp.

Read the clues. Each answer is a word from the story.
Write one letter on each line.
The letters in the boxes will spell another word from the story.

1. Another word for one dollar   — — ☐ —

2. The number of mints in the U.S.   — — ☐ —

3. How much one buck
   hide was worth   — — — — — — — — ☐

4. A buck is a male _____ .   — — — ☐

5. All U.S. coins are made of this.   — ☐ — —

6. Places where coins are made   — — ☐ — —

7. Dimes, pennies, and nickels are _____ .   ☐ — — — —

8. To buy things, we use _____ .   — — — — ☐

The word in the boxes is — — — — — — — — .

It is another word for: **deer**   **dollars**   **money**

Funny Money

Read each riddle.
Use the word box to help you solve each one.

1. What kind of money do astronauts have?

   _____ money!

2. What kind of money do kangaroos carry?

   _____ change!

3. Where does a horse go to get quick cash?

   _____ TM!

4. Why was the skunk sad?

   He didn't have a _____ on him!

5. What time is it when you give 4 boys 25 cents each?

   A _____ to four!

WORD Box ▶▶▶▶

hay	scent	pocket
quarter	launch	

U.S. Facts & Fun • EMC 6305 • ©2005 by Evan-Moor Corp.

Coin Purses

Uh oh, the money fell out of each purse!
Look at the amount written under each purse.
Find the group of coins that go with each purse.
Draw a line from the coins to the purse.

95¢

78¢

42¢

55¢

A $100 Coin

Design your own $100 coin.

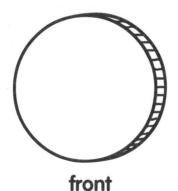
front

back

BEN AND THE BACKSTROKE

Long ago, few people knew how to swim. Almost no one had a swimming pool. Only the wealthy went to the seashore. Little Ben Franklin wanted to learn. But who could teach him?

Ben taught himself. He found a book called *The Art of Swimming.* He looked at the pictures. He read about diving. Soon, Ben was a great swimmer. He was an eager swimmer all of his life. Once he swam in the Thames River in England! Ben even taught some Englishmen to swim.

Back in America, Ben started a school. He made sure the students learned to swim, too. Maybe he wanted them to be above "C" level!

U.S. Facts & Fun • EMC 6305 • ©2005 by Evan-Moor Corp.

I KNOW THIS!

Have you heard the story of Ben's kite-flying experiment?
He found that lightning is electricity!
Read each question.
Draw a line from the bottom of the kite to the key with the correct answer.

Long ago, _____ people knew how to swim.

Ben Franklin was _____ when he learned to swim.

At Ben's _____ , he made sure students learned to swim.

Only the _____ went to the seashore.

Ben learned to swim from a _____ .

 wealthy

 book

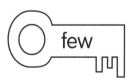 few

 school

 young

BACKWARDS BEN

Ben Franklin had a printing business. In those days, printers worked with raised letters on wooden blocks. The letters and words were backwards. When the blocks were inked and pressed onto paper, the words came out the right way.

Look at the words below. They are all backwards! Write them the right way. They are some of Ben's most famous words!

backwards

Time is money.

_____

Waste not, want not.

_____

There are no gains without pains.

_____

NEWSPAPER MAN

Ben Franklin started a newspaper. It was one of the best newspapers in the colonies. It was also the first newspaper to have cartoons!

Look at the cartoons below.
Fill in the bubbles to make the cartoons "talk."

"TREE" HOUSES

Have you ever been in a treehouse? Long ago, almost all houses were "tree" houses. They were log cabins!

People had to make houses from materials they could find. Big trees were all around. The trees were cut down with axes. Men cut pieces from each end. The logs fit together to make a square house. Mud was put between the logs to seal the cabin. The house had few windows.

Most log cabins had just one room. A big fireplace kept the cabin warm. Women cooked over the fire. Large families lived in these small homes. "Wood" you like to live in a house like this?

NO TRESPASSIN'

U.S. Facts & Fun • EMC 6305 • ©2005 by Evan-Moor Corp.

Read each silly sentence.
One word in each sentence is wrong.
The correct answer rhymes with it.
Circle the wrong word. Write the correct word on the line.

1　Long ago, most houses were bee houses.　＿＿＿＿＿＿＿＿＿

2　Wig trees were all around.　＿＿＿＿＿＿＿＿＿

3　Men cut down trees with waxes.　＿＿＿＿＿＿＿＿＿

4　Mud was put between the logs to heal the cabin.　＿＿＿＿＿＿＿＿＿

5　Most log cabins had just one bloom.　＿＿＿＿＿＿＿＿＿

6　Women cooked over a tire.　＿＿＿＿＿＿＿＿＿

 LOG PILES

Read the word above the top log.
How many smaller words can you make from it?
Write each new word on a log below it.

fireplace

cabins

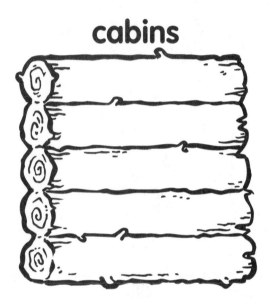

window

pioneer

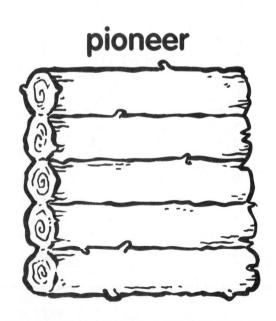

Crazy COLONIAL CABIN

It's 1750. This is a typical log cabin of that time. There are 6 things wrong with this picture. Circle each one.

Pucker Up, Prairie Pups!

Prairie dogs live on the prairie in the western U.S. But prairie dogs are not dogs. They are related to squirrels.

Prairie dogs live in underground burrows. One area of burrows is called a town. About a dozen prairie dogs live in one town.

Prairie dogs are not friendly to strangers. These animals have sharp teeth. They use them to bite outsiders.

But prairie pups are very friendly to others in their town. They even kiss each other! They cuddle up, too. Prairie dogs like to play with their friends. Sometimes they go together to find food. Would that be a puckering prairie pups' picnic?

U.S. Facts & Fun • EMC 6305 • ©2005 by Evan-Moor Corp.

Read each clue.
Find the prairie dog with the correct answer.
Draw a line from the clue to the prairie dog.

1. Prairie dogs live in this part of the U.S.

2. Prairie dogs are related to this animal.

3. A group of underground burrows is called this.

4. A stranger might get this from a prairie dog.

5. This is how a prairie dog greets a friend.

Safe at Home

This prairie pup is far from home.
Help him find his way.
Follow the tunnels to his burrow.

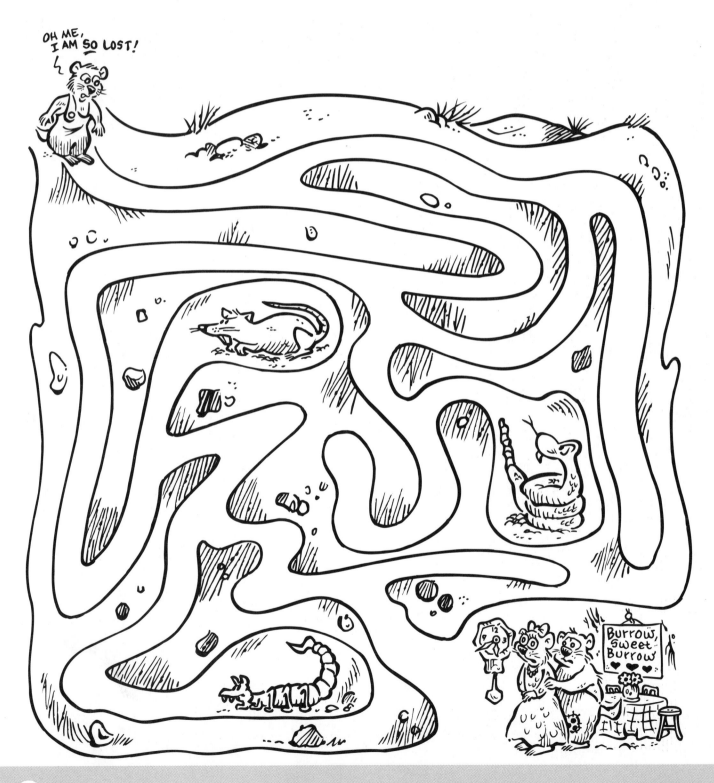

U.S. Facts & Fun • EMC 6305 • ©2005 by Evan-Moor Corp.

Secret Hiding Place

Solve each clue.
Write the word in the blanks.
When you are finished, read the word spelled out in the squares.

It will answer this question:

Where do you find a pup that puckers up?

Young prairie dogs are called ___ . ▪ ___ ___ ___

They live in underground ___ . ___ ___ ___ ▪ ___ ___

Their teeth are very ___ . ___ ___ ▪ ___ ___

They greet each other with a ___ . ___ ▪ ___

They are related to the ___ . ___ ___ ___ ___ ▪ ___ ___

They might ___ a stranger. ___ ▪ ___

They live in the ___ U.S. ___ ___ ___ ___ ▪ ___ ___

Answer: ☐ ☐ ☐ ☐ ☐ ☐ ☐

A Boy and a Balloon

What do Baltimore, a balloon, and a boy have in common? Read more and you will find out!

In 1783, most people traveled on foot or by horseback. That same year in France, the first hot-air balloon was launched. Its passengers were a duck, a sheep, and a rooster. Would people be able to fly next?

In Baltimore, a man named Peter Carnes built a hot-air balloon. Then he built bigger ones. Finally, he made a 35-foot balloon. Nearby, 13-year-old Edward Warren watched. He wanted to ride.

On June 24, 1784, Edward got his chance. A grown man was too heavy to go up. Edward was just the right size. Young Edward got into the basket. A rope kept the balloon from flying away from Baltimore. Edward was the first person in America to ride in a hot-air balloon!

U.S. Facts & Fun • EMC 6305 • ©2005 by Evan-Moor Corp.

Match the word or date with its correct clue.
Draw a line from the word to its answer.

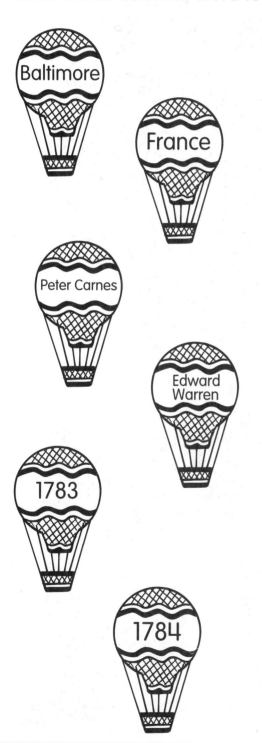

- the year the hot-air balloon was invented

- the young man who rode a balloon above Baltimore

- the city where the first U.S. hot-air balloon was made

- the maker of the first U.S. hot-air balloon

- the country where the first hot-air balloon was made

- the year the first hot-air balloon was launched in America

Beautiful Balloon

Hot-air balloons are colorful.
They have lots of different pictures and designs on them.
Color this one.
Draw yourself riding in the basket!

U.S. Facts & Fun • EMC 6305 • ©2005 by Evan-Moor Corp.

Hot-Air
Hidden Words

Circle each hidden word.
Cross it off the list.

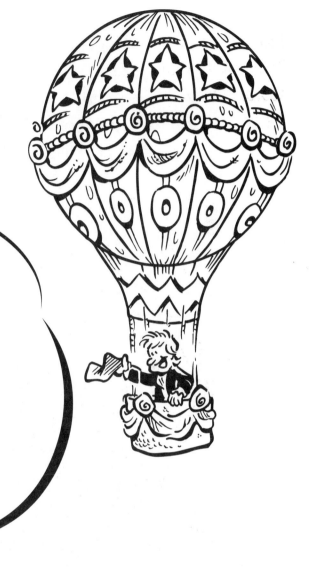

```
B   F   L   Y   B   M   F
A   H   O   T   A   I   R
L   I   N   C   S   P   A
L   G   Q   R   K   E   N
O   H   S   A   E   T   C
O   S   K   Y   T   E   E
N   E   D   W   A   R   D
```

high	hot	balloon	Peter
fly	air	basket	
sky	France	Edward	

SIGN UP HERE!

Have you ever been on a long trip? Did you stop along the way? Did you sign your name in a motel guest book? People on the Oregon Trail did. But they didn't write in a book. They carved or painted their names on a huge rock. We can still read their names today.

Independence Rock is the most famous rock along the Oregon Trail. It is in the middle of Wyoming. Most of the pioneers heading west stopped here. Some think that the rock was named when some travelers stopped there on July 4, 1841. No one really knows. We do know that many people passed this way.

I KNOW THIS!

Read each question.
Find the answer on the rock below.
Write the answer on the line.

1. Where is Independence Rock? _____

2. What was the name of one of the westward trails? _____

3. How did some travelers mark their names in the stone? _____

4. When might the rock have gotten its name? _____

5. Can the names be seen today? _____

ROCK Art

Some Native Americans drew pictures on Independence Rock.
Look at each drawing.
Label it with the correct word from the list.
Then color the art.

Word List

corn   turtle   woman
sun   river   man
fish   eagle   buffalo

Independence Rock

NAME GAME

Some names of places and people are hidden below.
Circle each one.
Cross off the name from the list.

```
B  L  Q  J  W  J  A  N  E  C
P  O  L  L  Y  W  E  H  P  O
M  I  S  S  O  U  R  I  E  L
O  C  T  Y  M  X  J  E  W  O
J  U  S  Z  I  D  O  M  I  R
A  E  A  K  N  S  H  A  L  A
M  O  R  E  G  O  N  R  L  D
E  F  A  V  A  E  M  Y  I  O
S  T  H  O  M  A  S  I  A  G
A  B  I  G  A  I  L  R  M  N
```

WORD Box ▷ ▷ ▷ ▷

Missouri	Sarah	James
Jane	Wyoming	Oregon
John	Thomas	Mary
Colorado	Abigail	William
Polly		

Blue Jean King: Levi Strauss

Gold Rush miners were tough on their pants. Bending and digging made their pants wear out quickly. What could they do? They needed sturdy trousers that would last a long time.

Levi Strauss heard the complaints. He owned a store in San Francisco. The store sold cloth and many other items. Strauss decided to make some new pants. He used the kind of canvas found on covered wagons. Another man, Jacob Davis, had an idea, too. He added metal rivets, or fasteners, to spots that tore easily.

The new pants were just right! The miners bought them. They happily paid 22 cents for a pair of Levi's jeans.

U.S. Facts & Fun • EMC 6305 • ©2005 by Evan-Moor Corp.

Read each sentence.
Choose the answer that best completes the sentence.
Circle the rivet next to the answer.

1. Gold Rush miners were tough on their _____ .
   - hats
   - pants
   - shovels

2. Levi Strauss _____ .
   - ignored the miners
   - disliked the miners
   - listened to the miners

3. Levi Strauss owned a store in _____ .
   - San Francisco
   - New Mexico
   - San Diego

4. Levi Strauss made new pants from fabric found _____ .
   - in China
   - among Native American tribes
   - on covered wagons

Look at each half below.
Read the word on each.
Match the left side of the pants with its right side.

Gold

Strauss

blue

Davis

Levi

Rush

Jacob

rivets

metal

jeans

U.S. Facts & Fun • EMC 6305 • ©2005 by Evan-Moor Corp.

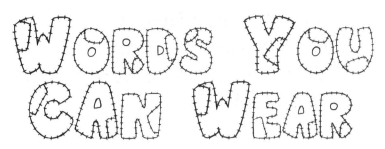

Some jobs need special clothes.
Read each job below.
Think about what you would wear
if you had that job.
Find the word below. Write it on
the line.

1 doctor

_____

2 farmer

_____

3 lifeguard

_____

4 police officer

_____

5 cook

_____

6 astronaut

_____

Chocolate Town, USA

Would you like to live in a town with its own chocolate factory? Welcome to Hershey, Pennsylvania!

In 1903, Milton S. Hershey built the first modern chocolate factory. Then he built a town around it. Hershey, Pennsylvania, was born! Workers liked living there. Today, the town has a zoo, a park, a theater, and a theme park. Streetlights are shaped like Hershey's Kisses. Hershey is the sweetest place on Earth!

I wonder…Do Hershey's cows give chocolate milk?

Read each sentence.
Color in the "Kiss" with the correct answer.

1. He built the first modern chocolate factory.

   Mr. Nestle   Mr. Penn   Mr. Hershey

2. The town was built first and then the factory.

    true   false

3. The "sweetest place on Earth" is in this state.

  New York   Pennsylvania   Florida

4. City streetlights are shaped like _____ .

  candy bars   gumdrops   chocolate
                                 Kisses

Sweet Treats

Americans love candy! Here are some riddles about candy.
Draw a line to the correct candy to solve each riddle.

1. I was invented when someone made a mistake, or "fudged," a batch of candy.

2. People used to chew beeswax. Now they chew me!

3. I am made of spun sugar and food coloring.

4. I am a "roll" named after my maker's daughter.

5. I cost just a cent in the early 1900s.

6. People in Vermont used me to make candy instead of sugar!

 penny candy

 Tootsie Roll

 maple syrup

 cotton candy

 fudge

 gumballs

U.S. Facts & Fun • EMC 6305 • ©2005 by Evan-Moor Corp.

Melt-in-Your-Mouth Maze

Little Milton Hershey lost his chocolate bar.
Help him find his way to it.

HERSHEY

WINTER RACES

Take a lot of snow and ice. Add sleds, sled dogs, and people. Now you have it—The Iditarod, "The Last Great Race on Earth!"

The first race was not planned. It was an emergency! Many sick people in Nome, Alaska, needed help. The closest medicine was in Anchorage. That was about 1,000 miles away. Twenty volunteers drove their dog sleds to deliver it. One by one, they handed off the medicine. A famous sled dog, Balto, was part of this team. The medicine arrived in Nome in only five days. The town was saved!

Today, the Iditarod Sled Dog Race is run every winter. Mush, dogs, mush!

Read each clue. Each answer is a word from the story.
Write one letter on each line.
The letters in the boxes will spell another word from the story.

1. The first race was ____ days long.

2. These are the real heroes.

3. This was delivered just in time.

4. The number of volunteers in the first race

5. A famous sled dog in the first race

6. The beginning city of the race

7. The ending city of the race

8. People ride these during the race.

The word in the boxes is _____ _____ _____ _____ _____ _____ _____ _____.

Box ▶ ▶ ▶ ▶ Anchorage   Balto   dogs   twenty
              medicine   sleds   five   Nome

TO THE RESCUE!

Connect the dots to find an important part of the race.
Color it.

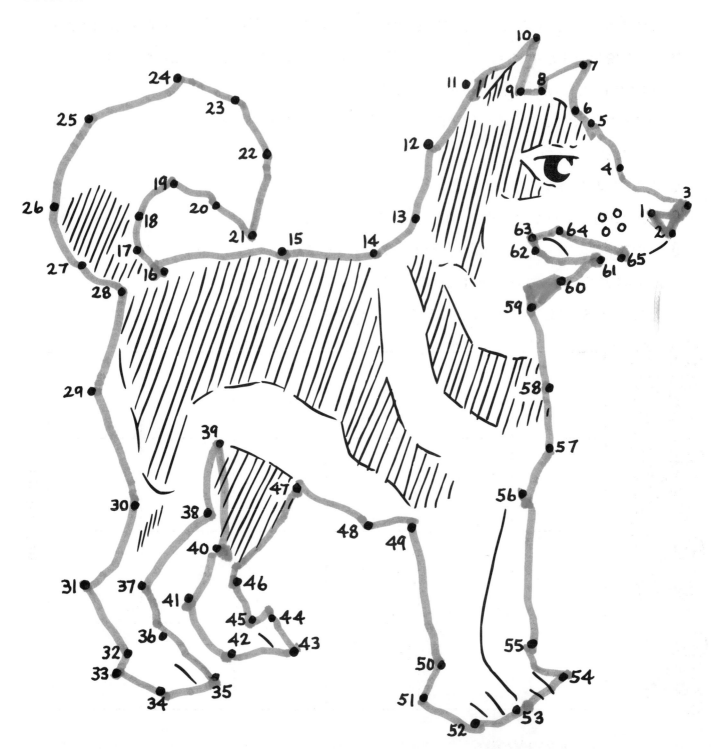

U.S. Facts & Fun • EMC 6305 • ©2005 by Evan-Moor Corp.

Along the IDITAROD TRAIL

These dogs are ready to race!
Read each line.
Color the squares to move each dog as it says.
Find out which dog wins the race.

1. Hotfoot, Digger, and Stormy get a head start. Move them forward one.
2. Digger stops to dig a hole. Hotfoot and Stormy move ahead one.
3. Nugget is coming! Move him ahead one.
4. Hotfoot stops to scratch his ear. Move Stormy ahead one.
5. Digger and Nugget dig in. Move them ahead two.
6. Stormy gets nervous. Move ahead one.
7. Hotfoot smells a rabbit. He doesn't move.
8. Nugget sees the finish. Move ahead two.
9. Digger catches up with Stormy.
10. Stormy stops to snap at Digger. Digger rushes ahead two.

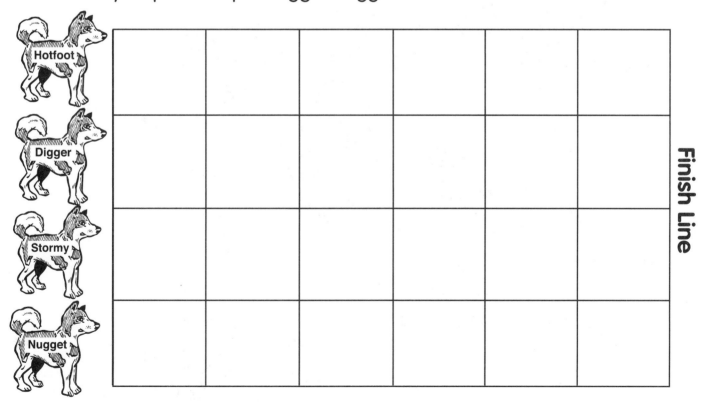

Who won?_____

House on Fire!

The summer of 1814 was hot and steamy. We were at war with the British. Our troops had fought for two years. At one time, the U.S. Army had burned some buildings in Canada. Now the British wanted to burn U.S. buildings.

They came to Washington, D.C. First, they set fire to the Capitol Building. Next, the British marched down Pennsylvania Avenue to the White House! Everyone quickly fled. Inside, the British found a meal all ready for 40 people. They ate it. Then they set fire to the White House.

A storm came at midnight. It put out the fire. The White House walls stood. After the war, the White House was rebuilt—and made whiter than ever!

U.S. Facts & Fun • EMC 6305 • ©2005 by Evan-Moor Corp.

Read each sentence.
Fill in the blank with a word or words from the word box.

1. In 1812, we were at war with the _____ .

2. The U.S. Army had burned buildings in _____ .

3. British troops set fire first to the _____ Building.

4. Then they moved toward the _____ .

5. Before they set the fire, they _____ .

6. A _____ came at midnight.

Capitol	storm	British
Canada	ate	White House

A Few More Facts

Here are more facts about the White House.
Read each clue.
Use the code to tell you what letters to write.

a = 1	e = 5	j = 10	n = 14	r = 18	v = 22
c = 3	h = 8	l = 12	o = 15	s = 19	w = 23
d = 4	I = 9	m = 13	p = 16	t = 20	y = 25

1. He was the first president to live in the White House.

☐ ☐ ☐ ☐ ☐ ☐ ☐ ☐ ☐
10 15 8 14   1 4 1 13 19

2. President Jackson fed some visitors a 1,400-pound block of this.

☐ ☐ ☐ ☐ ☐ ☐
3 8 5 5 19 5

3. The president's office is in this wing.

☐ ☐ ☐ ☐
23 5 19 20

4. It takes 570 gallons of this to cover the outside of the White House.

☐ ☐ ☐ ☐ ☐
16 1 9 14 20

5. This president made the name "White House" official in 1901.

☐ ☐ ☐ ☐ ☐
20 5 4 4 25

☐ ☐ ☐ ☐ ☐ ☐ ☐ ☐ ☐
18 15 15 19 5 22 5 12 20

My House ★ and the ★ White House

The White House is big!
What is your house like?
Fill in the chart to compare your house with the White House.
Then write in how many of each you want to have in your dream house.

	The White House	My House	My Dream House
Rooms	132		
Halls	40		
Bathrooms	32		
Levels (stories)	6		
Doors	412		
Fireplaces	28		
Bowling lanes	2		
Swimming pools	1		

Draw your dream house on the back of this page.

The Missing Cliff People

The place where the states of Colorado, Utah, New Mexico, and Arizona touch is called the Four Corners. If you go there, you can see old villages. They were built hundreds of years ago. Some things about the people who built these old villages is a mystery.

These people were called the Anasazi. The Anasazi built their homes high in the cliffs. They could see enemies coming from far away. The homes were made of poles and mud. These peaceful people farmed in the valley. They made beautiful pottery. And then they disappeared.

About 800 years ago, the Anasazi left their homes. Perhaps their water supply dried up. Maybe they were chased away by enemies. No one knows for sure. What do you think happened?

Read each sentence.
Choose the word or words that best complete each sentence.
Circle the answer.

1 The Anasazi built their homes in the _____ .

     valley   river   cliffs

2 They did <u>not</u> live in _____ .

     California   Arizona   Colorado

3 Their homes were made of poles and _____ .

     leaves   wood   mud

4 They _____ in the valley.

     died   farmed   herded cattle

5 About 800 years ago, the Anasazi _____ .

     grew stronger   disappeared   were discovered

Pueblo Pottery

Today's Pueblo tribes are probably descendants of the Anasazi. The Pueblo make beautiful pottery. They use patterns, like on the pottery below. Color this one. Then make your own design on the other one.

U.S. Facts & Fun • EMC 6305 • ©2005 by Evan-Moor Corp.

Triangle Maze

Triangles and circles were common designs of the Pueblo.
Follow the maze to find out which gateway leads to the Anasazi sun in
the middle.

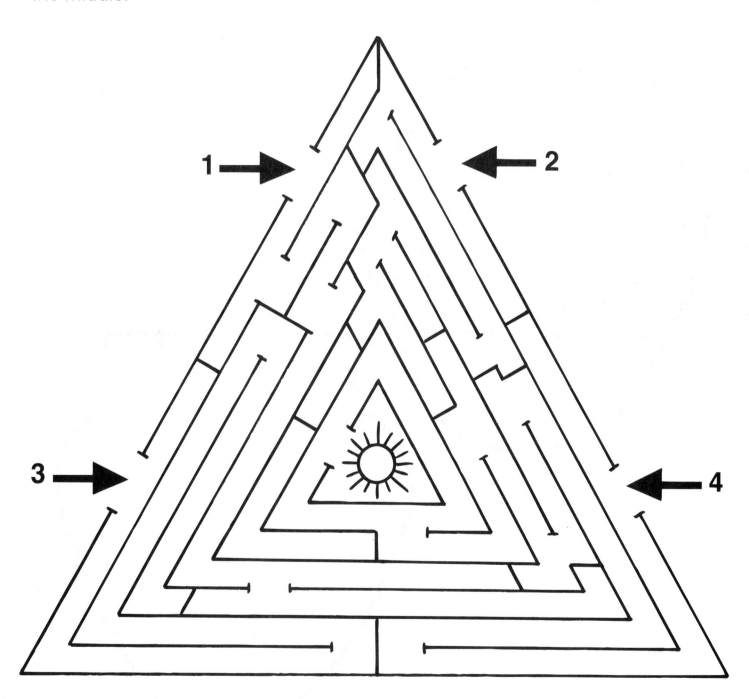

Lewis and Clark and Friend

   Lewis and Clark were great explorers. In 1803, they left Pittsburgh and headed west. They knew to take along many things on their long trip. Captain Lewis took along his dog, Seaman. Clark wrote all about the trip.

   Seaman was a black Newfoundland. This is a large dog that is strong and swims well. He would be a good friend along the trail. Once a Shawnee brave offered Lewis three beaver skins for the dog. Native Americans valued a good dog. Lewis kept Seaman. He also knew he had a good dog.

   Seaman helped catch food, usually squirrels. He warned the men of bears and buffalo. Seaman really was "man's best friend."

U.S. Facts & Fun • EMC 6305 • ©2005 by Evan-Moor Corp.

Read each clue.
Draw a line from the clue to its answer.

1. What are Lewis and Clark known for?

• Newfoundland

2. To whom did Seaman belong?

• exploring the West

3. Who wrote about the trip?

• squirrels

4. What kind of dog was Seaman?

• Lewis

• beaver skins

5. What does this kind of dog do well?

• Clark

6. What did a Shawnee brave offer for the dog?

• swims

7. What did Seaman catch for food?

Dog Facts

Unscramble the word to finish each dog fact.

1. Dogs only sweat from the bottoms of their **tefe**. _____

2. Dalmatians are born all **tihwe**. No spots! _____

3. Newfoundlands have webbed feet to help them **msiw**. _____

4. Don't **mesil** at a strange dog. It might think you are showing your teeth to start a fight! _____

5. A greyhound can **nru** up to 42 mph. _____

6. All puppies are born **dlinb** and deaf. They will begin to see and hear at about two weeks old. _____

U.S. Facts & Fun • EMC 6305 • ©2005 by Evan-Moor Corp.

Name That Dog

Color each dog.
Think of a name for each one.
Write the name on the tag.
Draw a line from the dog to its tag.

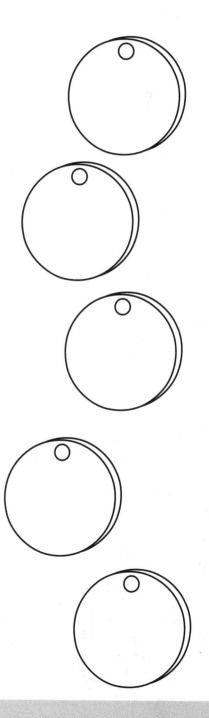

A Star Is Born

In 1776, the United States was a new country. It needed a new flag. George Washington called on his friend Betsy Ross. They went to the same church. Mrs. Ross had stitched shirts for him. Washington knew she was a good seamstress.

Washington and two other men visited Betsy Ross. They showed her a drawing of the flag they wanted. It had stars and stripes. The stars had 6 points. Betsy thought a 5-pointed star looked better. She showed them how easy it was to make one. First, she folded a piece of paper. She folded it many times. Then she made one cut—snip! Betsy unfolded the cut paper. It was a perfect 5-pointed star! The men liked it and agreed it should be on the flag. A U.S. star was born!

U.S. Facts & Fun • EMC 6305 • ©2005 by Evan-Moor Corp.

Read each sentence.
Find the missing word in one of the star's points.
Color the answer that completes each question.

1   George Washington and Betsy Ross went to the same ___ .
    Color the answer BLUE.

2   Betsy had stitched ___ for Washington.
    Color the answer RED.

3   Washington asked Betsy to make a ___ .
    Color the answer WHITE.

4   Washington's stars had ___ points.
    Color the answer YELLOW.

5   With one snip, Betsy made a star
    with ___ points.
    Color the answer GREEN.

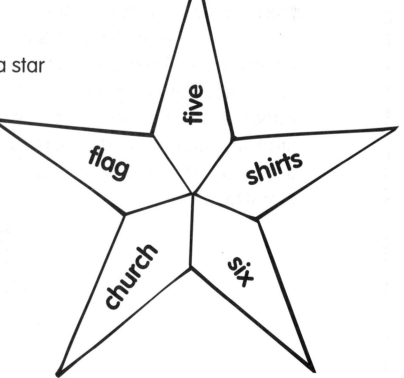

Make a Star

You can make a star just like Betsy Ross did. Have an adult help you. Follow these steps:

1. Start with a half sheet of copier paper. Fold in half and label corners **A, B, C, D** as shown.

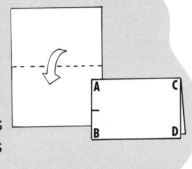

2. Locate the center of edge labeled **A-B** and mark with pencil. Fold **C** to this point.

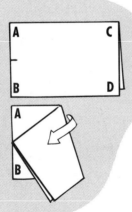

3. Fold flap **A** down as shown.

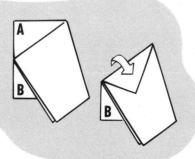

4. Fold bottom right up to meet top left edge.

5. Rotate shape upward to look like an ice-cream cone. Mark 1.4 cm from bottom point on the left side. Mark 3.3 cm from bottom point on the right side. Draw a line between these points. Cut on the line.

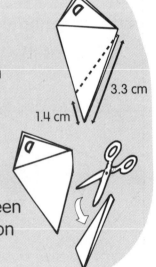

3.3 cm

1.4 cm

6. Unfold the small piece that was cut away. This is the star.

U.S. Facts & Fun • EMC 6305 • ©2005 by Evan-Moor Corp.

Red, White, & Blue Clues

Color the **R** areas red.
Color the **B** areas blue.
Leave the **W** areas white.

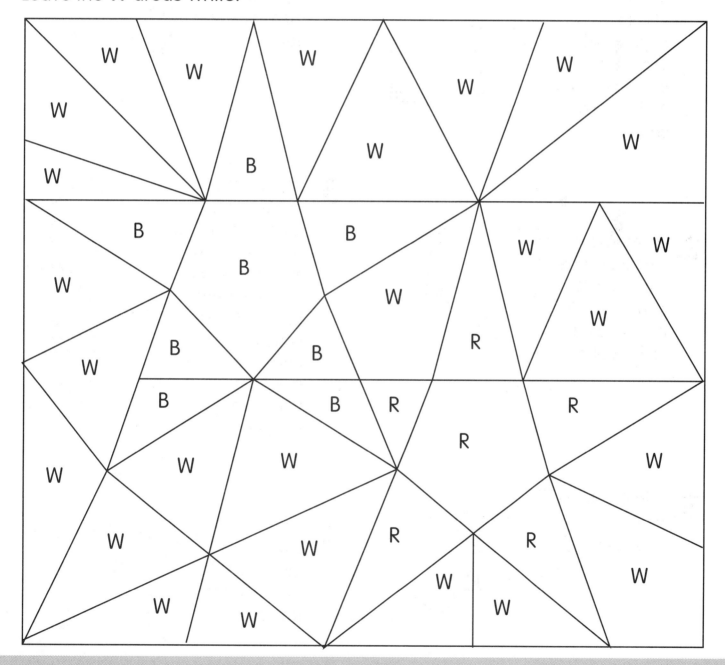

"WHOA!"
Special Delivery

"Giddy up, horsey!" Does that sound like your mail carrier? In 1860, it might have! Men on horses brought the mail. They rode from Missouri to California. This was called the Pony Express.

People in California waited a long time for their mail. Mail from the East traveled by ship around South America. It took months! Then someone had a good idea. Let's send mail by horse!

The Pony Express began in April 1860. The first letter came in only 10 days! More and more people used the Pony Express. But it cost $5.00 for one letter!

Then the telegraph was invented. It was faster and cheaper. In October 1861, the Pony Express ended.

U.S. Facts & Fun • EMC 6305 • ©2005 by Evan-Moor Corp.

Read each question.
Draw a line to the mail pouch with the correct answer.

1. When did the Pony Express begin?

2. When did the Pony Express end?

3. Where did the Pony Express take place?

4. How was mail sent before the Pony Express?

5. What replaced the Pony Express?

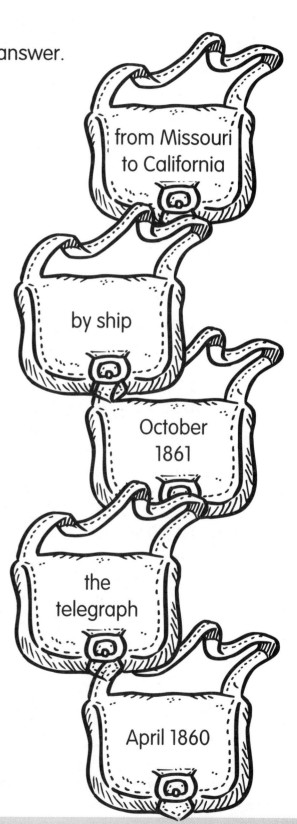

from Missouri to California

by ship

October 1861

the telegraph

April 1860

MAIL CALL!

Here are more Pony Express facts!
Unscramble the bold words.
Write the words on the envelopes.

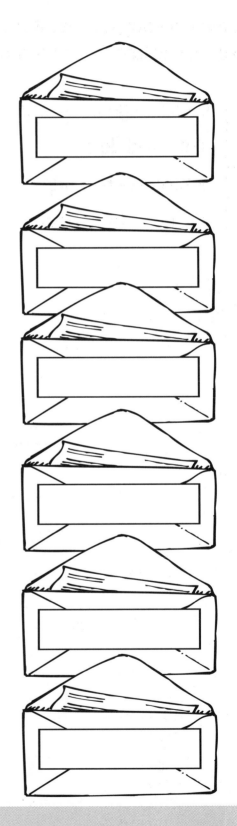

1. The Pony Express ran night and **yda**.

2. A Pony Express **dreir** made $100 a month.

3. Each rider rode about 60 **lsmie**.

4. A horse ran about 10 miles per **uorh**.

5. About 400 **srsohe** were used.

6. A rider had to weigh **sels** than 125 pounds.

U.S. Facts & Fun • EMC 6305 • ©2005 by Evan-Moor Corp.

PONY EXPRESS MAP

Follow the Pony Express through eight states.
Color each state. Then number them in "route" order, east to west.

- ☐ Nevada - green stripes
- ☐ Utah - red dots
- ☐ Nebraska - red stripes
- ☐ Missouri - blue stripes

- ☐ Kansas - orange dots
- ☐ California - blue dots
- ☐ Colorado - green dots
- ☐ Wyoming - orange stripes

A GIRL AND HER GUN

Annie Oakley was poor. She was born in 1860 in Ohio. Her mother did not have much money. Annie lived in a children's home for many years. When Annie was older, she went back home. She could help her family.

Annie liked to hunt. She was a good shot! She hunted food for her family. She hunted squirrels and rabbits. Annie sold some of the animals. She made a lot of money. Annie paid off her mother's home!

Annie entered contests. She did trick shots and almost never missed! Annie was better than most of the men. As an adult, she traveled and showed her skills. A Native American named Sitting Bull called her "Little Sure Shot."

U.S. Facts & Fun • EMC 6305 • ©2005 by Evan-Moor Corp.

Read each sentence.
Fill in the bull's-eye if it is true.
Mark an **X** on the outside ring if it is false.

	HIT	MISS
1 Little Annie Oakley was poor.	◎	◎
2 She never left her family.	◎	◎
3 Annie helped her family.	◎	◎
4 She planted a garden for food.	◎	◎
5 Annie sang to earn money.	◎	◎
6 She was a better shot than most men.	◎	◎
7 Her nickname was "Girl with a Gun."	◎	◎

A GIRL AND HER GUN

Annie has to practice shooting.
Can you help her?
Get Annie through the maze from her house
to the target area.

U.S. Facts & Fun • EMC 6305 • ©2005 by Evan-Moor Corp.

Really
A TRICKY SHOT

Annie was known for her trick shooting. Find the answer to each problem. Then connect the answers in order in the picture to show how Annie's bullet traveled.

1. $4 + 4 + 4 - 6 + 2 =$ ☐

2. $10 - 5 - 4 + 7 - 3 =$ ☐

3. $1 + 2 + 3 + 4 + 5 + 6 =$ ☐

4. $10 + 10 + 10 + 10 - 20 - 8 + 7 =$ ☐

5. $12 - 7 + 6 + 3 - 5 =$ ☐

IDAHO'S HOT POTATOES

Mashed. Baked. Chips. Fries. Nothing is "hotter" than a good potato. Every U.S. state grows potatoes. But Idaho is on the top of the potato pile. About 1/3 of all U.S. potatoes are grown there.

Idaho has just the right stuff to grow potatoes. Its soil is the right kind. There is snow in the winter. When the snow melts in the spring, the cool water helps the plants grow. Water is important. A potato is more than 3/4 water!

In the U.S., the average person eats 137 pounds of potatoes every year. Many potatoes become French fries. The first U.S. French fries were served in the White House. President Jefferson really liked them! Do you?

U.S. Facts & Fun • EMC 6305 • ©2005 by Evan-Moor Corp.

Read each sentence.
Choose the word that best completes each one.
Color the potato in front of the answer.

1. _____ grows one-third of the U.S. potatoes.

 Utah   Florida   Idaho

2. Its _____ is just right.

 soil    butter   sand

3. A potato is three-fourths _____ .

 sugar   water    soil

4. In the U.S., the average person eats 137 _____ of potatoes a year.

 baskets   bites   pounds

5. The first U.S. French fries were served to President _____ .

 Lincoln   Washington   Jefferson

ONE POTATO, TWO POTATO...

Potatoes are good food!
You can cook them lots of ways.
Look at each picture.
Write the name on the line.

_____ _____ _____

How many other ways can you think of to serve potatoes? Write them here.

_____

_____

_____

_____

_____

U.S. Facts & Fun • EMC 6305 • ©2005 by Evan-Moor Corp.

POTATO JOKES

Read each joke.
Color the funny pictures.

Q: How does a potato say good-bye?

A: "Later, tater!"

Q: What does Santa Tater say?

A: Ida-ho-ho-ho!

Q: What do you call a potato at the ice rink?

A: A tater skater!

Q: What do you call a bad potato?

A: A spud dud!

Q: Why couldn't the little potato spell "Mississippi"?

A: Because he didn't have enough i's!

State Birds

Cactus Wren

Brown Pelican

Every U.S. state has birds. But did you know that each state has a state bird? Some state birds are little. The state bird of Arizona is the cactus wren. It is only about 4 inches long. Some state birds are big. The state bird of Louisiana is the brown pelican. It grows to be 41 inches long. Both of these birds are brown.

The most popular state bird is not brown. It is bright red! It is the cardinal. Seven states have it as their state bird. The male cardinal is red. The female cardinal is gray-brown with red marks on its tail and wings. Cardinals are about 9 inches long. In the 1800s, people kept them in cages as pets. Now they are all wild birds. They are free to fly wherever they want.

The cardinal is the state bird of Ohio, Kentucky, Illinois, Indiana, North Carolina, Virginia, and West Virginia.

U.S. Facts & Fun • EMC 6305 • ©2005 by Evan-Moor Corp.

Read each clue.
Write the missing answer to solve the puzzle.

Across

3. In the 1800s, people kept them in _____ as pets.
8. The state bird of Arizona is the cactus _____ .
9. Now cardinals are all _____ birds.

c a r d i n a l

Down

1. The state bird of Louisiana is the brown _____ .
2. _____ states have the cardinal as their state bird.
4. Each state has a state _____ .
5. The color of the most popular state bird is _____ .
6. The cardinal is about 9 inches _____ .
7. The cactus wren and the pelican are both _____ .

Beautiful Birds

Each of these is a state bird.
Can you find pictures of them in a book?
Color them as they actually look.

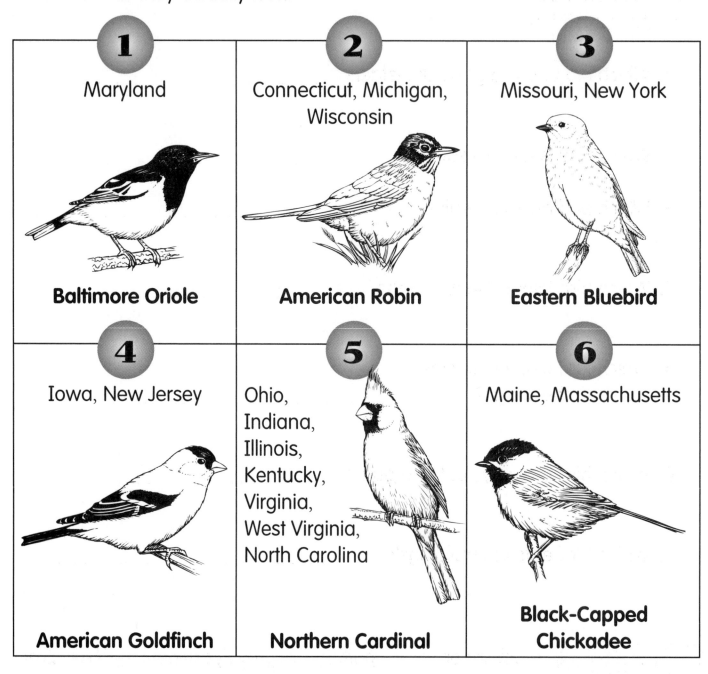

1 Maryland — **Baltimore Oriole**

2 Connecticut, Michigan, Wisconsin — **American Robin**

3 Missouri, New York — **Eastern Bluebird**

4 Iowa, New Jersey — **American Goldfinch**

5 Ohio, Indiana, Illinois, Kentucky, Virginia, West Virginia, North Carolina — **Northern Cardinal**

6 Maine, Massachusetts — **Black-Capped Chickadee**

What is your state bird? _____

U.S. Facts & Fun • EMC 6305 • ©2005 by Evan-Moor Corp.

Funny Feathered Friends

Read each riddle.
Find the answer below.
Write the correct bird on the line.

1. Which old bird is a good outfielder? _____

2. Which bird is always sad? _____

3. Which bird always steals? _____

4. Which bird joined the marathon? _____

5. Which bird didn't know the
   words to the songs? _____

6. Which bird is always out of breath? _____

7. Which bird eats big buildings? _____

| roadrunner | puffin | gray flycatcher | bluebird |
| hummingbird | robin | barn swallow | |

Wild Child

in the White House

Abraham Lincoln had four children. His youngest was named Thomas. Abe Lincoln called him "Tad." He said his son looked like a tadpole when he was a baby.

Tad was 8 years old when he moved into the White House. He loved to play tricks. Tad sprayed people with fire hoses. He locked doors. He rode a wagon through the White House. It was pulled by two goats!

Like his father, Tad cared about the soldiers. He had his own uniform. He sold food in the White House lobby to raise money for the army. Once he tried to sell his mother's clothes! He even sent care packages to the troops. Each was signed "a gift from Tad Lincoln."

FASTER, FASTER !!

Read each clue.
Decide if it is about Abe or Tad or both.
Circle the correct word.

1 _____ lived in the White House.

Abe   Tad   (both)

2 _____ said his son looked like a tadpole.

(Abe)   Tad   both

3 _____ sprayed people with fire hoses.

Abe   (Tad)   both

4 _____ cared about the Civil War soldiers.

Abe   Tad   (both)

5 _____ sold food to make money for the army.

Abe   (Tad)   both

6 _____ sent care packages to the troops.

Abe   (Tad)   both

Trouble in the White House

Tad is playing another trick!
He has brought some things into the White House.
Find each out-of-place item.
Circle it.
Then color the page.

How many silly things did you see?

Three-Letter Words

Read each clue.
Write the three-letter answer.
Finish each square.

1 across - Thomas's nickname
2 down - a small circle
3 across - a cat or dog is one
1 down - not the bottom

T	a	d
O	▓	
P		

4 across - Tad had a lot of this
5 down - you take one when tired
6 across - to tear something
4 down - not against

	▓	

7 across - Tad's dad
8 down - can be fried or scrambled
9 across - young Abe cut this
7 down - everything

		e
	▓	g
		g

10 across - father
11 down - to make a hole
12 across - a funny trick
10 down - grown-up puppy

	▓	

A BIG Gift

What is the biggest gift you ever got? America got a super-size gift in 1886. It was from France. The French admired America's freedom. So they gave us a present.

The gift was a statue. It was built in France. Then it was sent here piece by piece. It was put back together on an island in New York Harbor. The statue's name was "Liberty Enlightening the World." We call it the Statue of Liberty.

There are 354 steps inside the statue. In her crown there are 25 windows. Her fingernails are over a foot long. Now that's a big gift!

U.S. Facts & Fun • EMC 6305 • ©2005 by Evan-Moor Corp.

Read the clues.
Write the answers in the puzzle.

1 Starts with **F**
   In 1886, America got a gift from _____ .
   They admired America's _____ .

2 Starts with **S**
   It was the _____ of Liberty.
   There are 354 _____ inside the statue.

3 Starts with **W**
   There are 25 _____ in the crown.
   Its real name is "Liberty Enlightening the _____ ."

Our Symbol of Liberty

Label the parts of the Statue of Liberty.
Write a sentence at the bottom of the page to tell about the statue.

robe

tablet

base

crown

torch

_____

_____

U.S. Facts & Fun • EMC 6305 • ©2005 by Evan-Moor Corp.

Part by Part

Look at each clue.
Unscramble the letters to find the answer.
Write the answer on the lines.

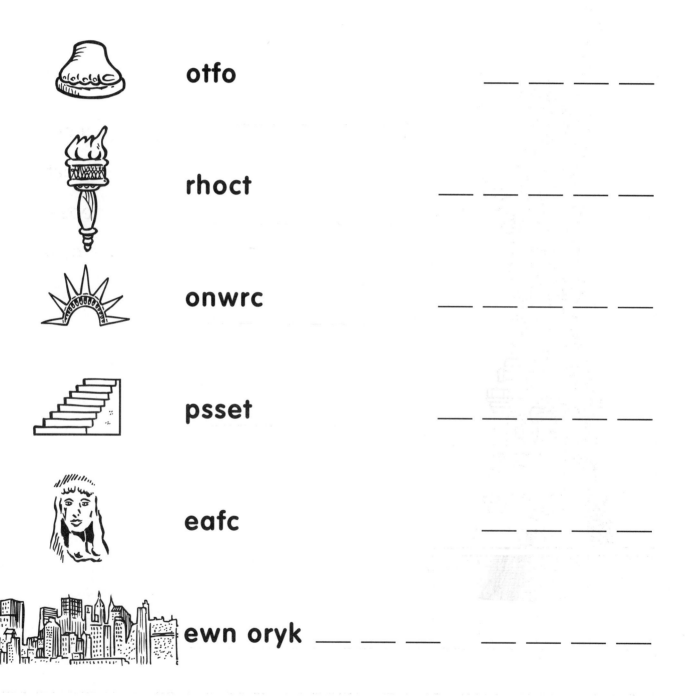

otfo   ___ ___ ___ ___

rhoct   ___ ___ ___ ___ ___

onwrc   ___ ___ ___ ___ ___

psset   ___ ___ ___ ___ ___

eafc   ___ ___ ___ ___

ewn oryk ___ ___ ___   ___ ___ ___ ___

Can You Hear Me Now?

You've seen the commercials. People call each other on the phone. And it doesn't matter how far away they are. To us, a phone call is no big deal.

In the 1870s, it was a big deal. People could not call each other. Instead, they had to send letters or a telegram. Telegrams were messages sent over wires using Morse code. Only one message could be sent at a time. It took a long time. But someone had a better idea.

Alexander Graham Bell studied sound. He made sound travel over wires. Bell made the first telephone in 1876. He was only 29 years old. Thanks to Bell, today you can ask someone in another country, "Can you hear me now?" and she will answer, "Yes, I can."

U.S. Facts & Fun • EMC 6305 • ©2005 by Evan-Moor Corp.

Read each sentence.
Draw a line to the word that best completes each sentence.

1. In the 1870s, people could not _____ each other.

2. They had to send letters or a _____ .

3. The telegraph used _____ code.

4. Only one _____ could be sent at a time.

5. Alexander Graham Bell made sound travel over _____ .

6. In 1876, he invented the _____ .

- Morse
- call
- wires
- telegram
- telephone
- message

Find the Phones

Find the eight phones in this picture.
Color each one.

U.S. Facts & Fun • EMC 6305 • ©2005 by Evan-Moor Corp.

Mr. Watson, Come Here!

The first words spoken over a telephone were, "Mr. Watson—come here—I want to see you."
Alexander Graham Bell was "calling" his assistant, Thomas Watson.

Help Mr. Bell's message get to Mr. Watson.

Mr. Watson . . .

Tornado Alley

Dorothy lived in Kansas. A big tornado took her to Oz. That story was not real. But tornadoes are real. And Kansas has a lot of them.

The middle part of the U.S. is called Tornado Alley. Every year, tornadoes touch down in these states. Moist air comes in from the Gulf of Mexico. Winds blow across the plains. When they get together, tornadoes are born.

Many states have tornadoes. But Tornado Alley is where the most tornadoes happen. The biggest ones happen there, too. Some twisters are more than a mile wide! They cause a lot of damage. Today, cities can warn people. Then they can be safe from the big spinning wind!

U.S. Facts & Fun • EMC 6305 • ©2005 by Evan-Moor Corp.

Read each sentence.
Choose the word that best completes it.
Circle the word.

1   The _____ part of the U.S. is called Tornado Alley.
     western   eastern   middle

2   _____ air comes in from the Gulf of Mexico.
     Dry   Moist   Cold

3   Winds blow across the _____ .
     plains   mountains   gulf

4   _____ states have tornadoes.
     Some   Many   All

5   Some twisters are more than a mile _____ .
     deep   wide   tall

6   People can be _____ from a tornado.
     safe   pulled   called

Weather Words

Look at each picture.
Put the weather word with the second word to make a new word.

 +  = __rain coat__

 +  = __Snow man__

 + = _____

 +  = _____

Draw a picture of one of the new words.

Storm Watch

The storm has blown the letters around!
Look at each picture.
Unscramble the letters.
Write the word in the blanks.
Color the pictures.

sown

___ ___ ___ ___

udclo

___ ___ ___ ___ ___

irna

___ ___ ___ ___

nyusn

___ ___ ___ ___ ___

A Ship's Best Friend

Do you have a night-light? So do ships at sea! They are called lighthouses. Ships can find their way home in the dark or in bad weather. America's first lighthouse was built in 1716. It was in Boston Harbor. It is not a working lighthouse now.

But some old lighthouses are still working. The Sandy Hook, New Jersey, lighthouse is more than 200 years old. It still lights up the night. One famous old lighthouse is the Statue of Liberty. It was the very first electric lighthouse. More than 1,500 lighthouses have been built in the U.S. Not all of them are still used.

Tall or short, old or new, these "night-lights" are a ship's best friend!

Read each sentence.
Write **T** if it is true or **F** it is false.

1 Lighthouses help ships in bad weather. _____

2 The first U.S. lighthouse was built in 1776. _____

3 It still works today. _____

4 The lighthouse at Sandy Hook, _____
New Jersey, still works.

5 The Statue of Liberty is not a lighthouse. _____

6 The Statue of Liberty was the first lighthouse _____
to use electricity.

Connect the Dots

Connect the dots from **1** to **27**.
Color the picture you uncover.

U.S. Facts & Fun • EMC 6305 • ©2005 by Evan-Moor Corp.

Name That Lighthouse

Look at each picture clue below.
Find the name of the lighthouse.
Draw a line to the name.

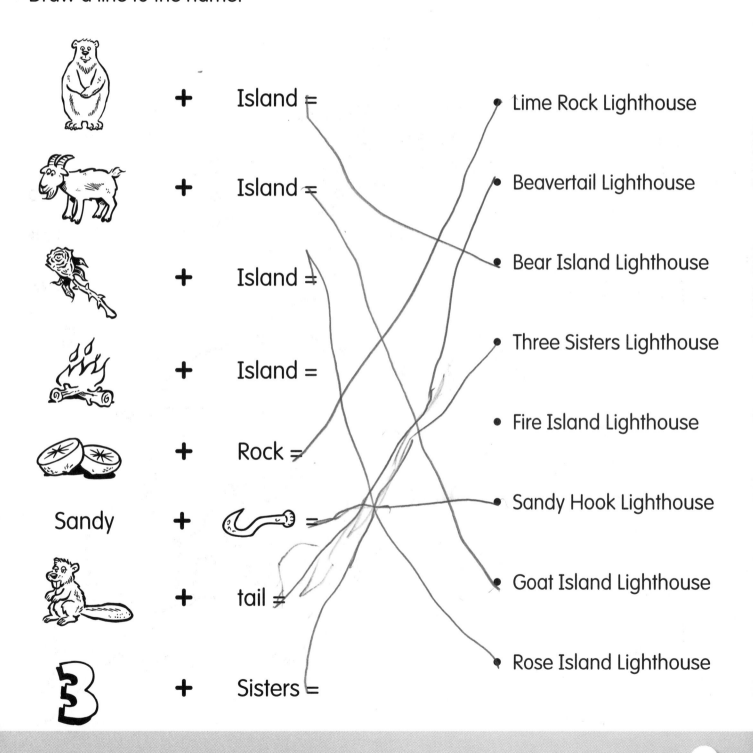

+ Island =   • Lime Rock Lighthouse

+ Island =   • Beavertail Lighthouse

+ Island =   • Bear Island Lighthouse

+ Island =   • Three Sisters Lighthouse

+ Rock =   • Fire Island Lighthouse

Sandy +   =   • Sandy Hook Lighthouse

+ tail =   • Goat Island Lighthouse

3 + Sisters = • Rose Island Lighthouse

FISH OVER THE FALLS

Niagara Falls is the second-largest area of waterfalls in the world. It is between Canada and the United States.

Niagara Falls is made up of two waterfalls, the American Falls and the Horseshoe Falls. The American Falls are in the U.S. state of New York. The Horseshoe Falls are in Ontario, Canada.

More than 750,000 gallons of water go over the falls each second. But that's not all that's falling over those falls. Fish fall over them, too! Do they die when they fall? Most of them live. They "go with the flow" and swim along. Some end up in Canada. Some end up in the United States. And they don't even need a passport!

U.S. Facts & Fun • EMC 6305 • ©2005 by Evan-Moor Corp.

Read the clues.
Write the answers in the puzzle.

1 Starts with **F**
These fall over the falls.
Niagara _____ is the second-largest area of waterfalls in the world.

2 Starts with **W**
More than 750,000 gallons of _____ go over the falls each second.
Niagara Falls is made up of two _____ .

3 Starts with **S**
They "go with the flow" and _____ along.
Some fish end up in the United _____ .

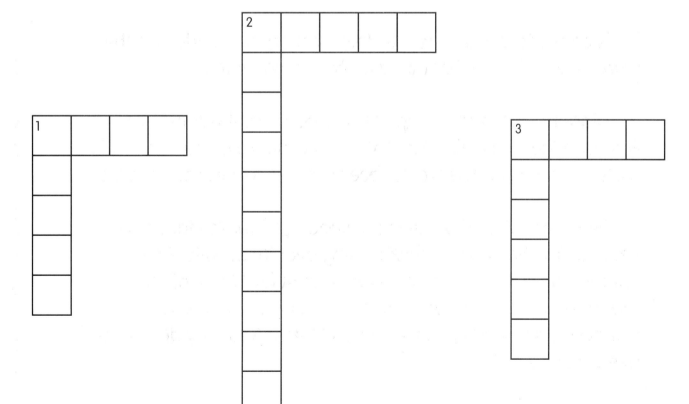

LET'S GO FISHING!

Many kinds of fish swim in the Niagara River between
Lake Erie and Lake Ontario.
Find the fish in the word search below.
Circle each one.

```
P E R C H B P W
I F C J Q H A A
K S A L M O N L
E U R Z W B B L
K G P L D A A E
T R O U T S S Y
M U S K I E S E
```

WORD Box ▶ ▶ ▶ ▶

bass	carp	pike	perch
trout	salmon	walleye	muskie

FISHY FUN

These fish are going over the Falls!
Find the one that is different. Circle it.

One Crack, Two Cracks, Three Cracks!

If something is broken, you might throw it away. Right? Not the Liberty Bell! It broke three times!

The first bell was made in England in 1752. It was a mix of copper and tin. The bell was sent to America. It cracked on its first ring. The bell was melted down and another bell was made. It cracked, too! Once more the bell was remade. In 1835, it was rung at a funeral. The bell cracked again! It was not fixed this time. The bell's crack was more than 24 inches long.

No one threw the bell away. In 1839, it was named the Liberty Bell. You can see it today in Philadelphia, Pennsylvania.

I KNOW THIS!

Read each sentence.
Color the bell beside the answer that best completes each sentence.

1 The Liberty Bell broke _____ times.

 2   3   5

2 The bell was first made in _____ .

 Philadelphia   New York   England

3 It was a mix of copper and _____ .

 tin   iron   silver

4 The last time it broke was during a _____ .

 funeral   parade   battle

5 You can see the Liberty Bell in _____ .

 Washington, D.C.   New York   Philadelphia

Cracked Picture

This picture is cracked up!
Something is hidden in it.
To find it, color the areas as follows:

B = blue   **E** = red   **L** = yellow

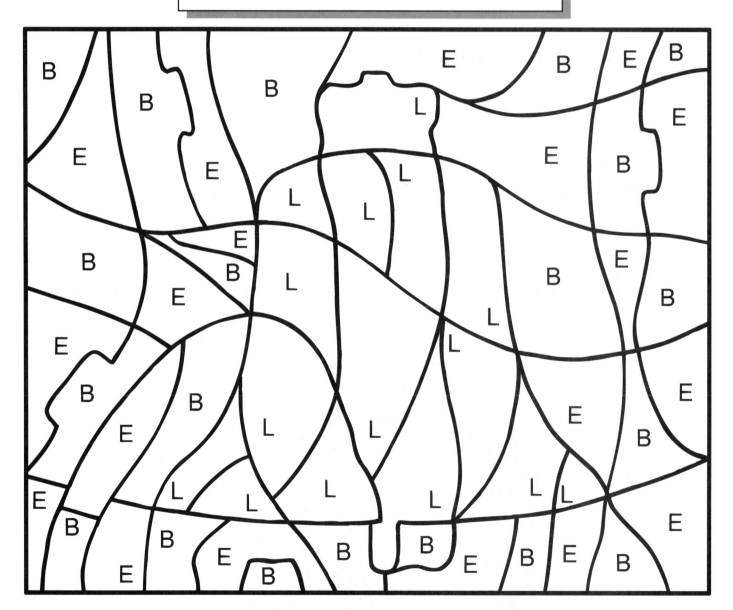

U.S. Facts & Fun • EMC 6305 • ©2005 by Evan-Moor Corp.

You Crack Me Up!

Read each riddle.
Draw a line to the best ending.

1. When should you ring
   the Liberty Bell?

   • He didn't have a
     very good "ring."

2. What did the people eat when
   they rang the Liberty Bell?

   • Crackers!

3. Why didn't the Liberty Bell ask the
   Blue Bell to marry him?

   • It cracks up!

4. What happens when you tell the
   Liberty Bell a joke?

   • At the "crack" of dawn.

JOHNNY, THAT ONE'S A SIDE SPLITTER!!

Buffalo Surprise

Buffaloes are big. They are the biggest land animals in North America. How could such a big animal surprise anyone? Just read this!

A buffalo is brown and tan. It has dark eyes, dark hooves, and a dark face. An adult can be 6 feet tall and weigh more than 2,000 pounds. That's a big, brown beast!

What if you saw one that was pure white? Would you be surprised? Well, meet White Cloud—a white buffalo.

White Cloud is very rare. She is an albino buffalo. Only one in 1 billion buffaloes is born like this. Native Americans believe a white buffalo is special. It stands for peace and hope.

U.S. Facts & Fun • EMC 6305 • ©2005 by Evan-Moor Corp.

Read each sentence.
Find the answer in the box.
Write the answer on the line.

1. The buffalo is the largest land animal in _____ .

2. A buffalo is brown and _____ .

3. An adult can be _____ feet tall.

4. It can weigh more than two _____ pounds.

5. White Cloud is a _____ buffalo.

6. Native Americans say she stands for peace and _____ .

| six | North America | white |
| tan | hope | thousand |

Missing Buffalo

Help the albino buffalo find his herd.

U.S. Facts & Fun • EMC 6305 • ©2005 by Evan-Moor Corp.

Buffalo Match-Up

Look at each picture.
Label each one.
Use the word box for help.
Then color each picture.

_____

_____

_____

_____

_____

_____

WORD Box ▶▶▶▶

Bridge with a Lid

Most bridges today are made of steel. Many cars can cross on them at one time. But once, bridges were made of wood. They were built for one horse and buggy to cross at a time. Many of these wooden bridges were "covered" bridges.

What is a "covered" bridge? A covered bridge is a wood bridge with a roof. Being on a covered bridge feels like being in a tunnel. It is dark inside the bridge, and you can see light at the ends of it.

There are still more than 800 covered bridges all over America. They are common in Pennsylvania, Vermont, Ohio, Indiana, and Oregon. Covered bridges remind us of America's past. If you cross through a covered bridge, you almost expect to see a horse and buggy waiting on the other side!

U.S. Facts & Fun • EMC 6305 • ©2005 by Evan-Moor Corp.

Read each sentence.
Unscramble the word to complete the sentence.
Write the word on the line.

1 Covered bridges were made

of _____ .

odow

2 Being on a covered bridge feels like

being in a _____ .

lneunt

3 A covered bridge is a wood bridge

with a _____ .

froo

4 Today, bridges are made of iron

and _____ .

lstee

5 Covered bridges remind us of

America's _____ .

stap

Uncover the Covered Words

Look at each word below.
Part of the word is inside the bridge.
Find the word in the list below.
Write the missing letters on the bridge.

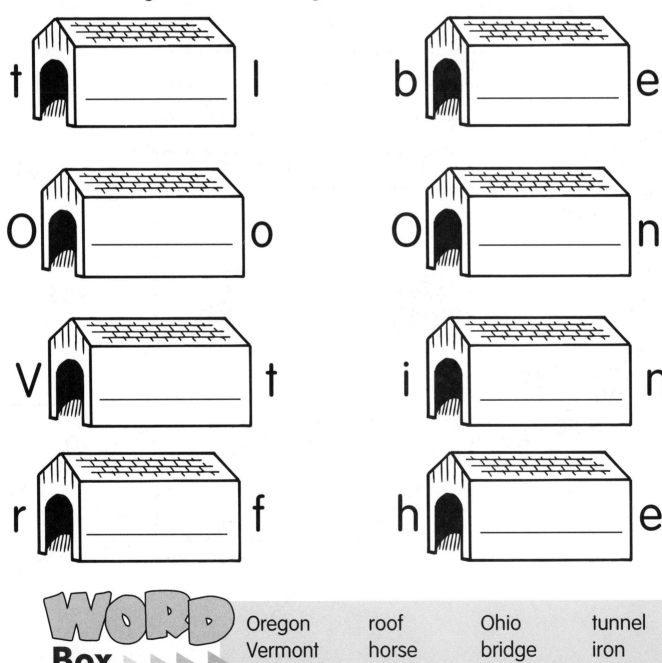

t _____ l

b _____ e

O _____ o

O _____ n

V _____ t

i _____ n

r _____ f

h _____ e

Help! Build a Bridge!

Farmer Brown wants to cross the river.
Connect the dots to help him.
Start at **5** and count by **5**s.

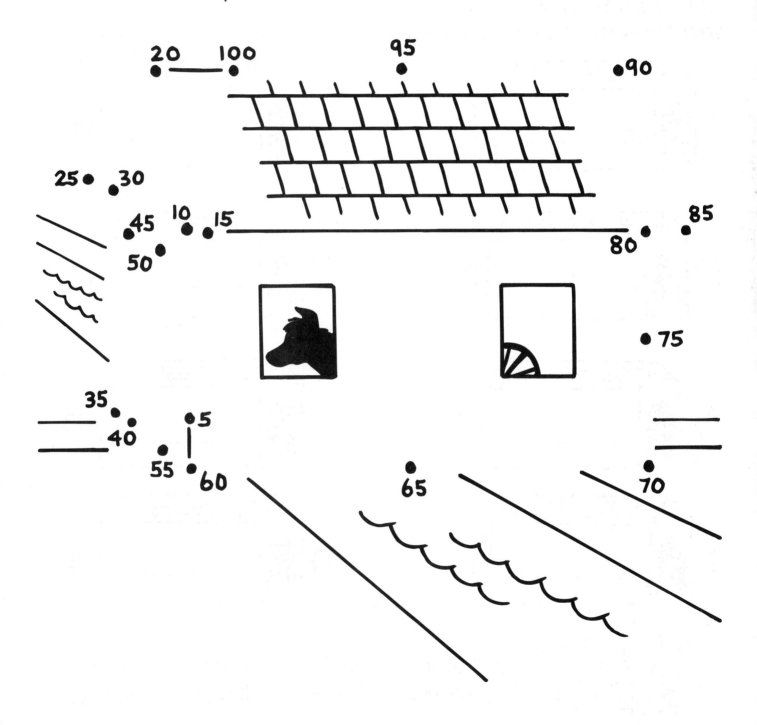

First to Fly

Do you get along with your brother or sister? Wilbur and Orville Wright had to. They worked together their whole lives.

After their schooling, they began to build things. Orville built a printing press. He and Wilbur wrote a weekly paper. Next, they built and sold bicycles. Wilbur and Orville saved the money they earned from their businesses. They both had big dreams. They wanted to fly.

They began to learn everything they could about flying. Soon, they built an airplane without a motor, called a glider. They built many gliders before they built one that flew. They believed in "try, try again!"

In 1902, the brothers started building a power airplane, a glider with a motor. They built plane after plane. Finally, in 1903 they built a plane that flew. It was in the air for 12 seconds. It only went 120 feet. But it flew! Their dream had come true.

Orville,
Don't forget
to write!!

WHEEEEEEEEEEEEE

U.S. Facts & Fun • EMC 6305 • ©2005 by Evan-Moor Corp.

Read each sentence.
Find the answer below.
Fill in the circle beside the "wright" answer.

1 The Wright brothers were named Wilbur and _____ .

O Otto   O William   O Orville

2 In their first business, they made a _____ .

O printing press   O bicycle   O glider

3 In their second business, they built and sold _____ .

O candy   O bicycles   O motors

4 They saved their money to build a _____ .

O printing press   O bicycle   O glider

5 In 1903, they flew for _____ seconds.

O 2   O 22   O 12

Just Alike

Find the two airplanes that are alike.
Color both of them the same.

U.S. Facts & Fun • EMC 6305 • ©2005 by Evan-Moor Corp.

My Own Shop

The Wright brothers had a bicycle shop.
What kind of shop would you like to have?
Finish the picture below to show your shop.
Give it a name.
Write about your shop on the lines below.

_____

_____

_____

_____

The
CAT IN THE HAT
Man

He wrote in the rain. He wrote on a train. He drew a hat. He drew a cat. Who was this man? He was Dr. Seuss, the man who wrote *The Cat in the Hat.*

Theodor Seuss Geisel (say gi-sell) was born in 1904—one hundred years ago! Little Ted (his nickname) loved to draw more than anything. He drew on his bedroom walls. He drew on his homework. He also loved to hear his mother tell rhymes. Ted lived near a zoo, too. Animals became his friends.

Ted became "Dr. Seuss" when he wrote books for children. Grown-ups like Dr. Seuss books, too. The next time you eat green eggs and ham, think of Dr. Seuss!

U.S. Facts & Fun • EMC 6305 • ©2005 by Evan-Moor Corp.

Read each sentence.
The missing word rhymes with the bold word.
Write the correct word on the line.

1. Dr. Seuss wrote children's _____ . **hooks**

2. His nickname was _____ Geisel. **Red**

3. He was born one hundred _____ ago. **fears**

4. He loved to _____ more than anything. **saw**

5. He lived near a _____ . **boo**

6. Dr. Seuss wrote *The Cat in the* _____ . **Mat**

DR. SEUSS'S COLORS

Dr. Seuss loved crayons.
He used colored pencils and markers, too.
His colors were bright.
Unscramble the color name on each crayon.
Then color each crayon the correct color.

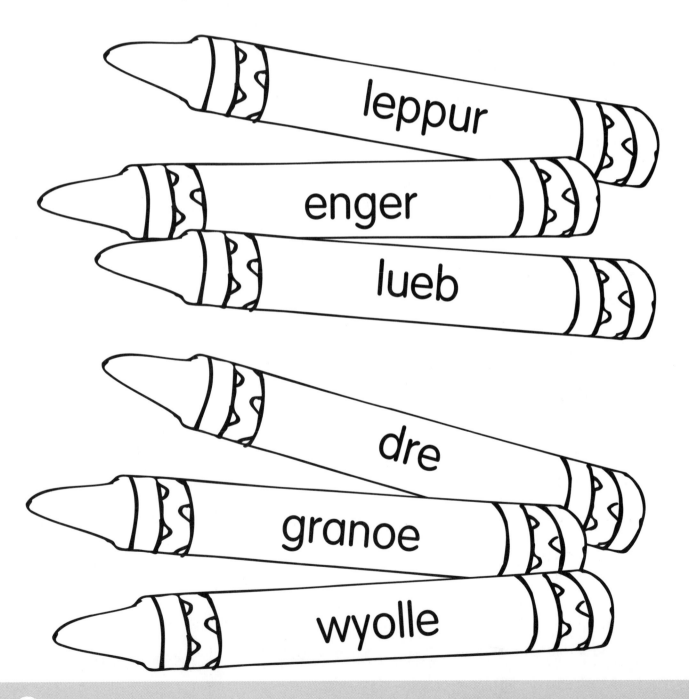

leppur

enger

lueb

dre

granoe

wyolle

ON A BOAT?
WITH A GOAT?

Fill in the blank with a word that rhymes with the bold word.
Use the picture clues.

1. I see a **sled**. It is under my _____ .

2. Go get that **dog**! He's chasing a _____ .

3. See that **cat**! It's sitting on my _____ .

4. We have a **pig**. It wears a _____ .

5. Look in my **mug**! I think it's a _____ .

Blowing Their Tops

Deep inside the Earth, it is very hot. It is so hot that rock melts! The melted rock is called magma. If cracks form in the Earth's surface, magma can flow up through the cracks. This is a volcano.

Whenever the magma comes out of the volcano, we say the volcano erupts. Sometimes the lava just seeps out of the volcano. Sometimes it explodes and shoots high into the air. Once the melted rock is outside the Earth, we call it lava.

The U.S. has many volcanoes. Most of them are in Hawaii, Alaska, and the western U.S. Most volcanoes don't erupt anymore. They are inactive.

But if a volcano does erupt, don't worry. We can tell if that's going to happen. Then people can get away safely.

Don't blow your top!

U.S. Facts & Fun • EMC 6305 • ©2005 by Evan-Moor Corp.

Read each sentence.
Decide if it is true or false.
If it is **true**, draw and color smoke coming from the volcano.
If it is **false**, leave the volcano "asleep."

1. The inside of the Earth is very cold.

2. Melted rock inside the Earth is called magma.

3. We never know when a volcano is going to erupt.

4. Volcanoes that erupt are inactive.

5. Many volcanoes are in the U.S.

New Volcano Is Made!

The pictures below show how a volcanic mountain may form. Find the explanation that matches each picture. Write the picture number in the circle. Then color the pictures.

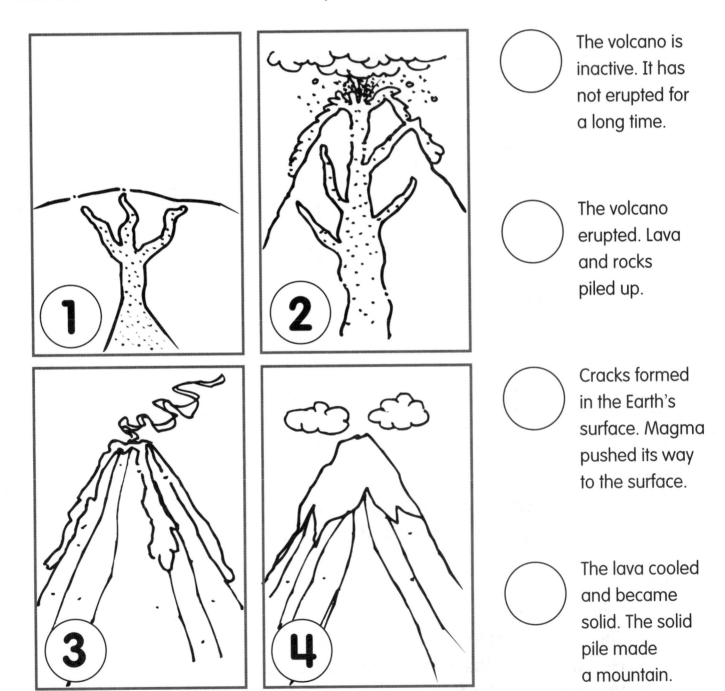

The volcano is inactive. It has not erupted for a long time.

The volcano erupted. Lava and rocks piled up.

Cracks formed in the Earth's surface. Magma pushed its way to the surface.

The lava cooled and became solid. The solid pile made a mountain.

U.S. Facts & Fun • EMC 6305 • ©2005 by Evan-Moor Corp.

Red-Hot Puzzle

Read each clue.
Write the answer in the puzzle.

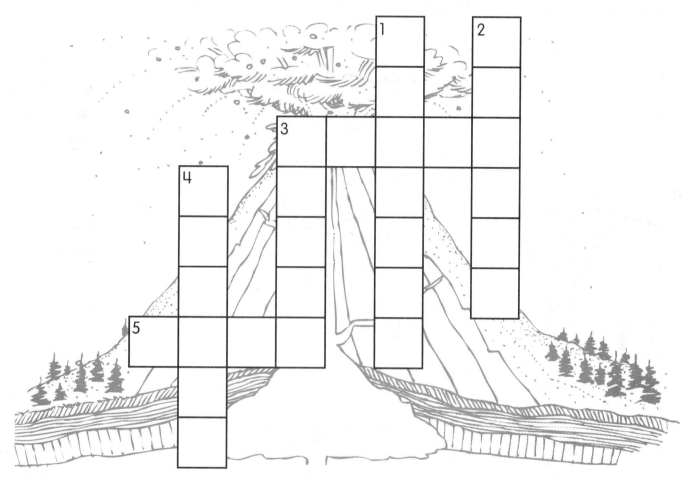

Across

3. Inside the Earth, rock is so hot that it _____ .
5. Hot _____ may come out of a volcano.

Down

1. When pressure builds up, a _____ erupts.
2. The _____ of the Earth is very hot.
3. Hot rock inside the Earth is called _____ .
4. Volcanoes can be found in _____ , Alaska, and the western U.S.

MAN OR MACHINE?

Have you ever used a hammer? Most people hammer nails into wood. John Henry hammered steel stakes into rock. It was his job. And he was the best.

In the 1870s, the railroad was growing. It was moving across our land to reach the West. Mountains got in the way sometimes. Then tunnels had to be dug through rock. John Henry and other hard workers pounded steel stakes into the rock to make holes. Black powder was put into the holes and lit. After the explosion, the big pieces of rock were hauled away. John Henry earned $1.25 a day for this dangerous work.

One day there was a contest. Who was faster—a machine drill or a man? The man was John Henry. The story says he beat the machine. He became a legend and a hero to hardworking people.

Read each sentence.
Find the missing word in the box below.
Write the word on the line.

1. In the 1870s, the _____ was growing.

2. John Henry hammered _____ stakes into rock.

3. The stakes made _____ where black powder was put.

4. After the explosion, the big pieces of _____ were hauled away.

5. The workers earned $1.25 a _____ .

6. One day there was a _____ .

7. The story says that John Henry beat a _____ .

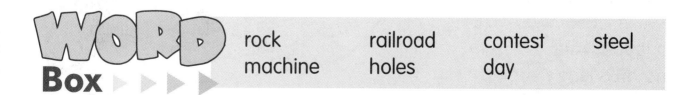

WORD Box ▶ ▶ ▶ ▶

rock	railroad	contest	steel
machine	holes	day	

BUILDING THE RAILROAD

Follow the maze to get to the next town.
Watch out for the big rocks!

STEEL DRIVIN' MAN

John Henry was called "The Steel Drivin' Man."
Find words about him in the word search.

```
J  O  H  N  S  D  T
M  H  E  N  R  Y  U
S  A  W  R  O  H  N
T  M  J  P  C  O  N
A  M  F  I  K  L  E
K  E  S  T  E  E  L
E  R  I  L  L  K  G
```

WORD Box ▶▶▶▶▶ steel   hammer   tunnel   John
                    Henry   rock   stake   hole

Deep Dark Cave

Mammoth means "big." Really, really big! Mammoth Cave is the biggest bunch of caves in the world. The caves go on for 335 miles! They are like deep, dark mazes.

The caves are home to many odd animals. There is almost no light in the caves. The animals cannot see much. Some of the fish have no eyes! Some spiders have no color. Cave crickets live there, too. Bats, rats, and frogs live in the caves part of the time.

Mammoth Cave National Park is in Kentucky. Thousands of people visit it every year. Don't worry about getting lost. They have park leaders to show you the way.

U.S. Facts & Fun • EMC 6305 •

Read the clues.
Write one letter on each line.
The letters in the boxes will spell another word from the story.

1. The caves are like deep, dark _____ .
2. Mammoth has the biggest bunch of _____ in the world.
3. They are _____ to many odd animals.
4. The caves go on for 335 _____ .
5. The cave spiders have no _____ .
6. Mammoth Cave National Park is in _____ .
7. There is almost no _____ in the caves.

___ ___ ___ ___ ___

___ ___ ___ ___ ___

___ ___ ___ ___

___ ___ ___ ___ ___

___ ___ ___ ___

___ ___ ___ ___ ___ ___

___ ___ ___ ___ ___

The word is the boxes is _____ .

It means _____ .   **dark**   **maze**   **big**

Hidden Animals

Mammoth Cave is home to many animals.
Unscramble the animal names below.
Find the animals in the cave and color them.

orgf _____   tab _____   tra _____

hifs _____   prised _____   tickerc _____

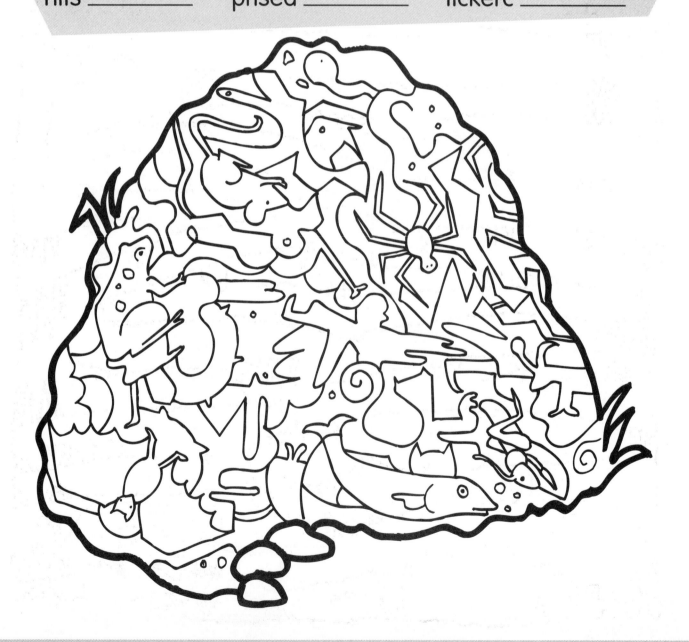

U.S. Facts & Fun • EMC 6305 • ©2005 by Evan-Moor Corp.

Cave Maze

Find your way through the cave maze.

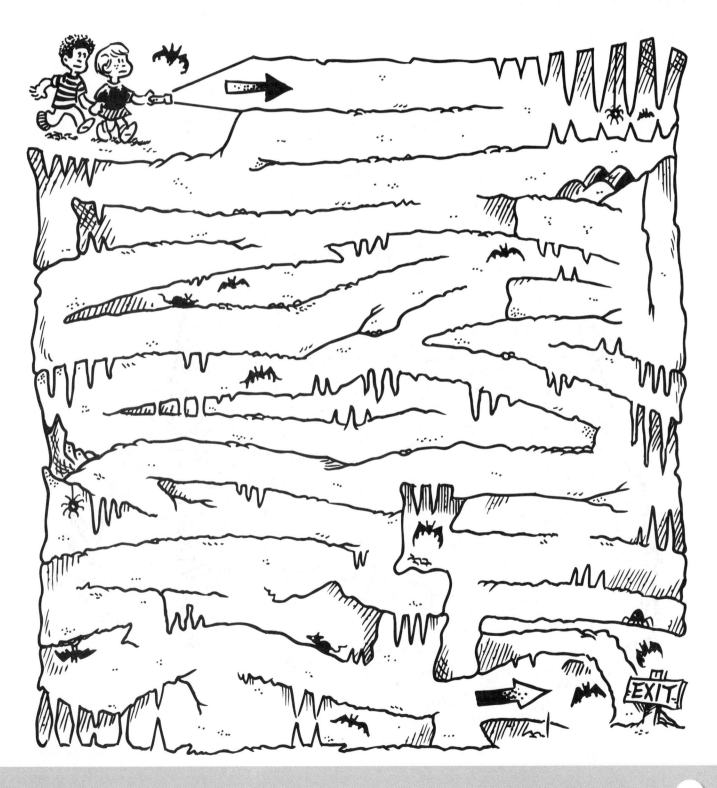

America's Weirdest Lake

Anyone can swim here because everyone can float!
The Great Salt Lake in Utah has the saltiest water in the U.S.
It is the second-saltiest body of water in the world. The saltier
the water, the better you can float. Just don't let the water get
in your eyes. Ouch!

All of Earth's oceans are made of salt water. But the Great
Salt Lake is even saltier than they are. Only special things can
live in this water. Brine shrimp, called sea monkeys, live there.
No fish live in the Great Salt Lake. It's too salty! But some tall
tales say that a sea monster lives in the lake. Maybe it's
a giant sea monkey!

U.S. Facts & Fun • EMC 6305 • ©2005 by Evan-Moor Corp.

Read each sentence.
Decide if it is true or false.
If the answer is **true,** color the lake blue.
If the answer is **false,** make an **X** on the lake.

1 Everyone can float in the Great Salt Lake.

true

false

2 It is the second-saltiest body of water in the U.S.

true

false

3 No fish live there.

true

false

4 The oceans are saltier than this lake.

true

false

5 Brine shrimp are also called sea donkeys.

true

false

6 The story of the sea monster is a tall tale.

true

false

Down by the Lake

You can see lots of things at the Great Salt Lake.
Animals and plants live there.
You can also see beautiful sunsets.
Use the words in the bubbles to complete the puzzle.
Hint: Start with the 5-, 6-, and 8-letter words.

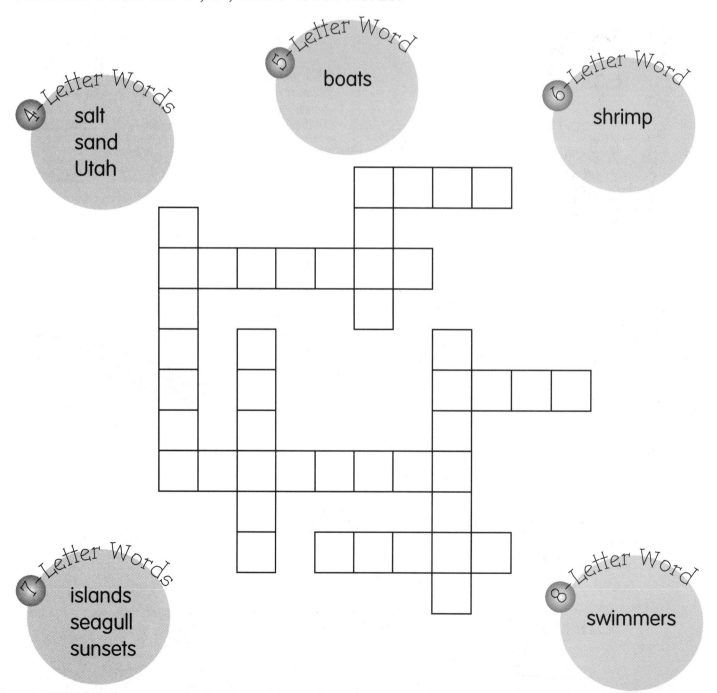

4-Letter Words
salt
sand
Utah

5-Letter Word
boats

6-Letter Word
shrimp

7-Letter Words
islands
seagull
sunsets

8-Letter Word
swimmers

U.S. Facts & Fun • EMC 6305 • ©2005 by Evan-Moor Corp.

Salty or Sweet?

Look at all this food!
Color the things that taste salty **yellow**.
Color the things that taste sweet **blue**.

Answer Key

Page 3

Page 4

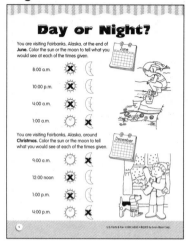

Page 5

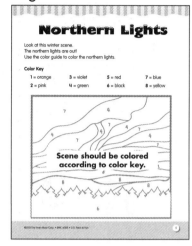

Page 7

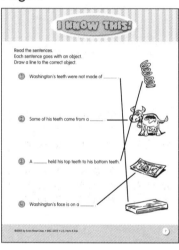

Page 8

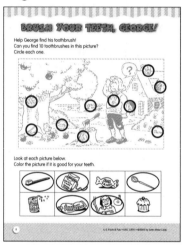

Page 9

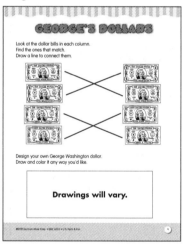

Page 11

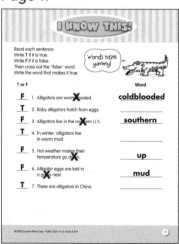

Page 12

Page 13

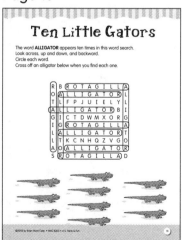

Page 15

I KNOW THIS!

Read each sentence.
Unscramble the bold word or number.
Write the word on the line.

1. James Marshall found **logd** at Sutter's Mill. — **gold**
2. The Gold Rush started in **8418**. — **1848**
3. Gold was in rivers and **csrok**. — **rocks**
4. The biggest piece was **915** pounds. — **195**
5. Now California is called the **ldonGe** State. — **Golden**
6. A lump of gold is called a **gungte**. — **nugget**

Page 16

RHYME TIME!

Read each riddle.
The two words in each answer will rhyme.

What is green and grows on nuggets?

g_old **m**_old

Where do gold diggers eat?

At the **m**_iner **d**_iner

Where do you dig for evergreen trees?

At a **p**_ine **m**_ine

Page 17

WHERE'S THE GOLD?

Color Key
G = gold (or yellow)
O = orange
L = lime green
D = dark blue

Something is hidden in this puzzle.
You can "mine" it by coloring the pieces.

Scene should be colored according to color key.

The hidden "gold" is the shape of _____ **California** _____!

Page 19

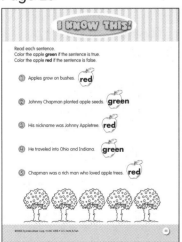

I KNOW THIS!

Read each sentence.
Choose the word or words that make the sentence true.
Write the word on the line.

1. Life on the prairie was **lonely**
   crowded   lonely   easy
2. Pioneer kids had to think up their own **games**
   chores   names   games
3. It was hard to play hide-and-seek because there were few **trees**
   buffalo   children   trees
4. Marbles sometimes were made of **dried clay**
   dried clay   sticks   cowhide
5. Dolls sometimes were made of **corn husks**
   plastic   corn husks   shoes

Page 20

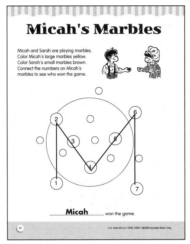

Micah's Marbles

Micah and Sarah are playing marbles.
Color Micah's large marbles yellow.
Color Sarah's small marbles brown.
Connect the numbers on Micah's marbles to see who won the game.

_____ **Micah** _____ won the game.

Page 21

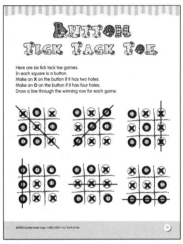

BUTTON TICK TACK TOE

Here are six tick tack toe games.
In each square is a button.
Make an **X** on the button if it has two holes.
Make an **O** on the button if it has four holes.
Draw a line through the winning row for each game.

Page 23

I KNOW THIS!

Read each sentence.
Color the apple **green** if the sentence is true.
Color the apple **red** if the sentence is false.

1. Apples grow on bushes. **red**
2. Johnny Chapman planted apple seeds. **green**
3. His nickname was Johnny Appletree. **red**
4. He traveled into Ohio and Indiana. **green**
5. Chapman was a rich man who loved apple trees. **red**

Page 24

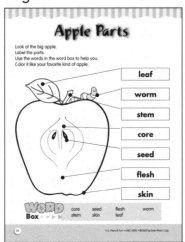

Apple Parts

Look at the big apple.
Label the parts.
Use the words in the word box to help you.
Color it like your favorite kind of apple.

leaf
worm
stem
core
seed
flesh
skin

WORD Box ▶▶▶ core   seed   flesh   worm
stem   skin   leaf

Page 25

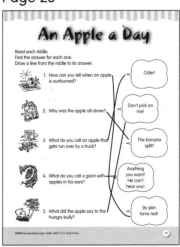

An Apple a Day

Read each riddle.
Find the answer for each one.
Draw a line from the riddle to its answer.

1. How can you tell when an apple is sunburned?
2. Why was the apple all alone?
3. What do you call an apple that gets run over by a truck?
4. What do you call a giant with apples in his ears?
5. What did the apple say to the hungry bully?

Cider!
Don't pick on me!
The banana split!
Anything you want! He can't hear you!
Its skin turns red!

Page 27

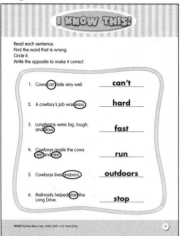

I KNOW THIS!

Read each sentence.
Find the word that is wrong.
Circle it.
Write the opposite to make it correct.

1. Cows can hide very well. — **can't**
2. A cowboy's job was easy. — **hard**
3. Longhorns were big, tough, and slow. — **fast**
4. Cowboys made the cows rest and rest. — **run**
5. Cowboys lived indoors. — **outdoors**
6. Railroads helped start the Long Drive. — **stop**

Page 28

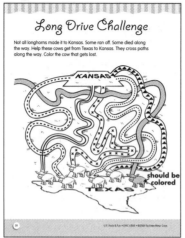

Long Drive Challenge

Not all longhorns made it to Kansas. Some ran off. Some died along the way. Help these cows get from Texas to Kansas. They cross paths along the way. Color the cow that gets lost.

should be colored

Page 29

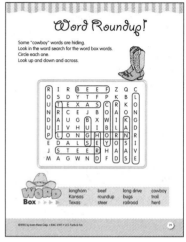

Word Roundup!

Some "cowboy" words are hiding.
Look in the word search for the word box words.
Circle each one.
Look up and down and across.

WORD Box

longhorn	beef	long drive	cowboy
Kansas	roundup	bugs	trail
Texas	steer	railroad	herd

Page 31

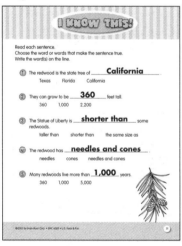

I KNOW THIS!

Read each sentence.
Choose the word or words that make the sentence true.
Write the word(s) on the line.

1. The redwood is the state tree of **California**.
   Texas   Florida   California
2. They can grow to be **360** feet tall.
   360   1,000   2,200
3. The Statue of Liberty is **shorter than** some redwoods.
   taller than   shorter than   the same size as
4. The redwood has **needles and cones**.
   needles   cones   needles and cones
5. Many redwoods live more than **1,000** years.
   360   1,000   5,000

Page 32

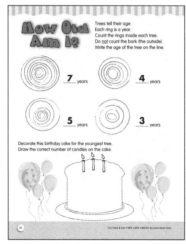

How Old Am I?

Trees tell their age.
Each ring is a year.
Count the rings inside each tree.
Do not count the bark (the outside).
Write the age of the tree on the line.

7 years   **4** years
5 years   **3** years

Decorate this birthday cake for the youngest tree.
Draw the correct number of candles on the cake.

Page 33

Forest Friends

Lots of animals live in the forest.
There are 10 hiding in the redwood trees.

Find each of the animals.
Color each animal.

Page 35

I KNOW THIS!

Read each sentence below.
Circle yes or no.

1. A roadrunner can run 15 miles per hour.   **yes**   no
2. Roadrunners are afraid of people.   yes   **no**
3. Roadrunners cannot fly.   yes   **no**
4. A roadrunner can catch a snake.   **yes**   no
5. Roadrunners can jump straight up.   **yes**   no

Page 36

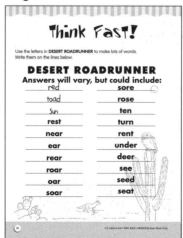

Think Fast!

Use the letters in DESERT ROADRUNNER to make lots of words.
Write them on the lines below.

DESERT ROADRUNNER
Answers will vary, but could include:

red	sore
toad	rose
sun	ten
rest	turn
near	rent
ear	under
rear	deer
roar	see
oar	seed
soar	seat

Page 37

Picture Words

Look at each pair of pictures.
Together, they make a new word.
Find that word in the box.
Write it on the line.

+ = **roadrunner**
+ = **rattlesnake**
+ = **butterfly**
+ = **cowboy**
+ = **anthill**
+ = **eggshell**

WORD Box

| anthill | cowboy | eggshell |
| rattlesnake | roadrunner | butterfly |

U.S. Facts & Fun • EMC 6305 • ©2005 by Evan-Moor Corp.

Page 39

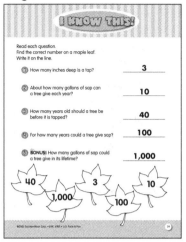

I KNOW THIS!

Read each question.
Find the correct number on a maple leaf.
Write it on the line.

1. How many inches deep is a tap? — **3**
2. About how many gallons of sap can a tree give each year? — **10**
3. How many years old should a tree be before it is tapped? — **40**
4. For how many years could a tree give sap? — **100**
5. **BONUS!** How many gallons of sap could a tree give in its lifetime? — **1,000**

Leaves: 40, 3, 10, 1,000, 100

Page 40

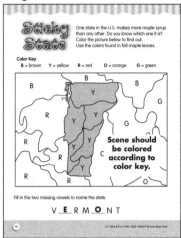

Sticky State

One state in the U.S. makes more maple syrup than any other. Do you know which one it is?
Color the picture below to find out.
Use the colors found in fall maple leaves.

Color Key
B = brown   Y = yellow   R = red   O = orange   G = green

Scene should be colored according to color key.

Fill in the two missing vowels to name the state.

V E R M O N T

Page 41

Wacky Waffle

Fill in the empty waffle squares. All but one of the words is from the story.
The squares will solve this riddle:

Where did the baker find his missing lid?

MAPLE
TAPPED
SPRING
CANDY
FARMER
BUCKET
SWEET

In the **pancake**.

Page 43

I KNOW THIS!

Read each sentence.
Does it tell about a turkey or an eagle?
Circle the turkey or eagle to show your answer.

1. Ben Franklin liked me best.
2. I like to eat seeds and bugs.
3. My feathers stand for bravery.
4. I was at the first Thanksgiving.
5. I am America's national bird.
6. I stand for peace and strength.

Page 44

Wacky Birds!

Look at the picture below.
What is wrong with these birds?
Fill in the blanks.

Turkeys...
can't hang **upside down**.
don't **swim**.
don't **eat** takeout.
don't wear **shoes**.
don't **read** newspapers.

Eagles...
aren't **afraid** of **mice**.
don't have **beaks** like toucans.
don't have **feathers** like peacocks.
don't eat **seeds**.
don't wear **wigs**.

Page 45

State Bird Words

Each state in the U.S. has a state bird.
Unscramble the bird word beside each state name. That's the state bird!

1. Minnesota — onlo — **loon**
2. Utah — sae lugl — **sea gull**
3. Louisiana — cpeinla — **pelican**
4. New Hampshire — leuprp nhfic — **purple finch**
5. Arizona — sucatc nwer — **cactus wren**
6. Connecticut, Michigan, and Wisconsin — inorb — **robin**
7. All of these states have this as their state bird:
   Illinois, Indiana, Kentucky, North Carolina, Ohio, Virginia, and West Virginia. — niraldca — **cardinal**

WORD Box
cardinal   loon   pelican   seagull
purple finch   cactus wren   robin

Page 47

I KNOW THIS!

Read each clue.
Write the answer in the puzzle.

s t a r s
t   r
r   e
white   b
p   Glory
e   l
s t a t e   u

Across
1. There are 50 _____ on the flag.
3. The color _____ stands for purity.
5. One name for the flag is "Old _____."
6. Each star stands for a _____.

Down
1. There are 13 _____ on the flag.
2. The color _____ stands for courage.
4. The color _____ stands for loyalty and friendship.

Page 48

How many STARS?

Count the stars on the United States flag.
Fill in your answers in the box below.
Color the flag.

There are **50** stars.
I see **5** rows with 6 ☆'s.
I see **4** rows with 5 ☆'s.

Page 49

MAKE YOUR FLAG

A flag stands for a country or a state.
Some flags stand for a person or an idea.
If you had a flag that shows something about you, what would it look like?
Draw your flag below.

Drawings will vary.

Page 51

I KNOW THIS!

Read the clues. Each answer is a word from the story.
Write one letter on each line.
The letters in the boxes will spell another word from the story.

1. Another word for one dollar — **b u c k**
2. The number of mints in the U.S. — **f o u r**
3. How much one buck hide was worth — **o n e d o l l a r**
4. A buck is a male _____. — **d e e r**
5. All U.S. coins are made of this. — **m e t a l**
6. Places where coins are made — **m i n t s**
7. Dimes, pennies, and nickels are _____. — **c o i n s**
8. To buy things, we use _____. — **m o n e y**

The word in the boxes is **c u r r e n c y**

It is another word for: deer   dollars   (money)

Page 52

Funny Money

Read each riddle.
Use the word box to help you solve each one.

1. What kind of money do astronauts have?
   launch (money)
2. What kind of money do kangaroos carry?
   pocket change!
3. Where does a horse go to get quick cash?
   hay TM!
4. Why was the skunk sad?
   He didn't have a **scent** on him!
5. What time is it when you give 4 boys 25 cents each?
   A **quarter** to four!

WORD Box ▸▸▸ hay   scent   pocket
                   quarter   launch

Page 53

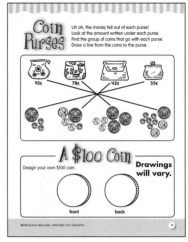

Coin Purses

Uh oh, the money fell out of each purse!
Look at the amount written under each purse.
Find the group of coins that go with each purse.
Draw a line from the coins to the purse.

95¢   78¢   42¢   55¢

A $100 Coin

Design your own $100 coin.

Drawings will vary.

front   back

Page 55

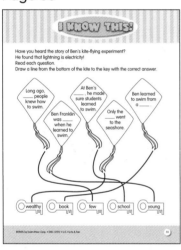

I KNOW THIS!

Have you heard the story of Ben's kite-flying experiment?
He found that lightning is electricity!
Read each question.
Draw a line from the bottom of the kite to the key with the correct answer.

- Long ago, _____ people knew how to swim.
- At Ben's _____, he made sure students learned to swim.
- Ben learned to swim from a _____.
- Ben Franklin was _____ when he learned to swim.
- Only the _____ went to the seashore.

wealthy   book   few   school   young

Page 56

BACKWARDS BEN

Ben Franklin had a printing business. In those days, printers worked with raised letters on wooden blocks. The letters and words were backwards. When the blocks were inked and pressed onto paper, the words came out the right way.

Look at the words below. They are all backwards! Write them the right way. They are some of Ben's most famous words!

backwards → **backwards**

Time is money.
Time is money.

Waste not, want not.
Waste not, want not.

There are no gains without pains.
There are no gains without pains.

Page 57

NEWSPAPER MAN

Ben Franklin started a newspaper. It was one of the best newspapers in the colonies. It was also the first newspaper to have cartoons!

Look at the cartoons below.
Fill in the bubbles to make the cartoons "talk."

Answers will vary.

Page 59

I KNOW THIS!

Read each silly sentence.
One word in each sentence is wrong.
The correct answer rhymes with it.
Circle the wrong word. Write the correct word on the line.

1. Long ago, most houses were (bee) houses. — **tree**
2. (Wig) trees were all around. — **Big**
3. Men cut down trees with (waxes). — **axes**
4. Mud was put between the logs to (heal) the cabin. — **seal**
5. Most log cabins just had one (bloom). — **room**
6. Women cooked over a (hire). — **fire**

Page 60

LOG PILES

Read the word above the top log.
How many smaller words can you make from it?
Write each new word on a log below it.

Answers will vary.

fireplace
fire   lace
place   rip
pace   lip
ace   pear
face   ear

cabins
can   cab
in   bin
ban   an
nab

window
wind   down
now   own
win   won
widow   on
wow   in

pioneer
pin   rope
peer   ripe
pore   rip
open   one
pen   on

Page 61

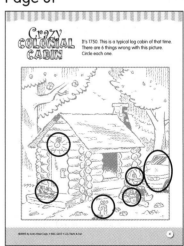

Crazy COLONIAL CABIN

It's 1750. This is a typical log cabin of that time.
There are 6 things wrong with this picture.
Circle each one.

Page 63

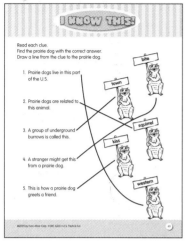

I KNOW THIS!

Read each clue.
Find the prairie dog with the correct answer.
Draw a line from the clue to the prairie dog.

1. Prairie dogs live in this part of the U.S.
2. Prairie dogs are related to this animal.
3. A group of underground burrows is called this.
4. A stranger might get this from a prairie dog.
5. This is how a prairie dog greets a friend.

bite, town, squirrel, kiss, western

Page 64

Safe at Home

This prairie pup is far from home.
Help him find his way.
Follow the tunnels to his burrow.

Page 65

Secret Hiding Place

Solve each clue.
Write the word in the blanks.
When you are finished, read the word spelled out in the squares.

It will answer this question:

Where do you find a pup that puckers up?

Young prairie dogs are called ____	p u p s
They live in underground ____	b u r r o w s
Their teeth are very ____	s h a r p
They greet each other with a ____	k i s s
They are related to the ____	s q u i r r e l
They might ____ a stranger.	b i t e
They live in the ____ U.S.	w e s t e r n

Answer: p r a i r i e

Page 67

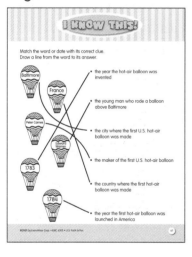

I KNOW THIS!

Match the word or date with its correct clue.
Draw a line from the word to its answer.

Baltimore
France
Peter Carnes
Edward Warren
1783
1784

- the year the hot-air balloon was invented
- the young man who rode a balloon above Baltimore
- the city where the first U.S. hot-air balloon was made
- the maker of the first U.S. hot-air balloon
- the country where the first hot-air balloon was made
- the year the first hot-air balloon was launched in America

Page 68

Beautiful Balloon

Hot-air balloons are colorful.
They have lots of different pictures and designs on them.
Color this one.
Draw yourself riding in the basket!

Drawings will vary.

Page 69

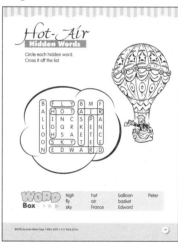

Hot-Air
Hidden Words

Circle each hidden word.
Cross it off the list.

Word Box
high   hot   balloon   Peter
fly   air   basket
sky   France Edward

Page 71

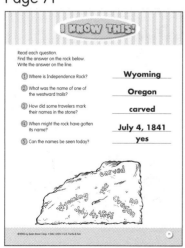

I KNOW THIS!

Read each question.
Find the answer on the rock below.
Write the answer on the line.

1. Where is Independence Rock? — **Wyoming**
2. What was the name of one of the westward trails? — **Oregon**
3. How did some travelers mark their names in the stone? — **carved**
4. When might the rock have gotten its name? — **July 4, 1841**
5. Can the names be seen today? — **yes**

Page 72

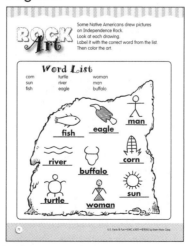

Rock Art

Some Native Americans drew pictures on Independence Rock.
Look at each drawing.
Label it with the correct word from the list.
Then color the art.

Word List
corn   turtle   woman
sun   river   man
fish   eagle   buffalo

man
fish   eagle
river   corn
buffalo
turtle woman sun

Page 73

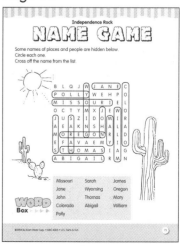

Independence Rock
NAME GAME

Some names of places and people are hidden below.
Circle each one.
Cross off the name from the list.

Word Box
Missouri   Sarah   James
Jane   Wyoming Oregon
John   Thomas   Mary
Colorado   Abigail William
Polly

Page 75

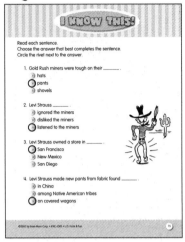

I KNOW THIS!

Read each sentence.
Choose the answer that best completes the sentence.
Circle the rivet next to the answer.

1. Gold Rush miners were tough on their _____ .
   - hats
   - ● pants
   - shovels

2. Levi Strauss _____ .
   - ignored the miners
   - disliked the miners
   - ● listened to the miners

3. Levi Strauss owned a store in _____ .
   - ● San Francisco
   - New Mexico
   - San Diego

4. Levi Strauss made new pants from fabric found _____ .
   - in China
   - among Native American tribes
   - ● on covered wagons

Page 76

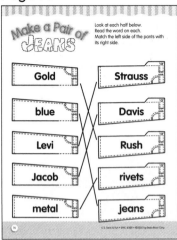

Make a Pair of JEANS

Look at each half below.
Read the word on each.
Match the left side of the pants with its right side.

Gold	Strauss
blue	Davis
Levi	Rush
Jacob	rivets
metal	jeans

Page 77

WORDS YOU CAN WEAR

Some jobs need special clothes.
Read each job below.
Think about what you would wear if you had that job.
Find the word below. Write it on the line.

1. doctor — scrubs
2. farmer — overalls
3. lifeguard — swimsuit
4. police officer — uniform
5. cook — apron
6. astronaut — spacesuit

WORD Box ▸ swimsuit apron uniform spacesuit overalls scrubs

Page 79

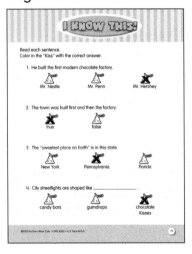

I KNOW THIS!

Read each sentence.
Color in the "Kiss" with the correct answer.

1. He built the first modern chocolate factory.
   - Mr. Nestle
   - Mr. Penn
   - ✗ Mr. Hershey

2. The town was built first and then the factory.
   - ✗ true
   - false

3. The "sweetest place on Earth" is in this state.
   - New York
   - ✗ Pennsylvania
   - Florida

4. City streetlights are shaped like _____ .
   - candy bars
   - gumdrops
   - ✗ chocolate Kisses

Page 80

Sweet Treats

Americans love candy! Here are some riddles about candy.
Draw a line to the correct candy to solve each riddle.

1. I was invented when someone made a mistake, or "fudged," a batch of candy.
2. People used to chew beeswax. Now they chew me!
3. I am made of spun sugar and food coloring.
4. I am a "roll" named after my maker's daughter.
5. I cost just a cent in the early 1900s.
6. People in Vermont used me to make candy instead of sugar!

- penny candy
- Tootsie Roll
- maple syrup
- cotton candy
- fudge
- gumballs

Page 81

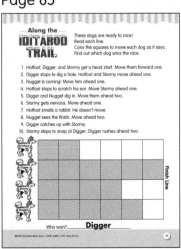

Melt-in-Your-Mouth Maze

Little Milton Hershey lost his chocolate bar.
Help him find his way to it.

HERSHEY

Page 83

I KNOW THIS!

Read each clue. Each answer is a word from the story.
Write one letter on each line.
The letters in the boxes will spell another word from the story.

1. The first race was ___ days long. **five**
2. These are the real heroes. **dogs**
3. This was delivered just in time. **medicine**
4. The number of volunteers in the first race **twenty**
5. A famous sled dog in the first race **Balto**
6. The beginning city of the race **Anchorage**
7. The ending city of the race **Nome**
8. People ride these during the race. **sleds**

The word in the boxes is **Iditarod**

WORD Box ▸ Anchorage Balto dogs twenty medicine sleds five Nome

Page 84

TO THE RESCUE!

Connect the dots to find an important part of the race.
Color it.

Page 85

Along the IDITAROD TRAIL

These dogs are ready to race!
Read each line.
Color the squares to move each dog as it says.
Find out which dog wins the race.

1. Hotfoot, Digger, and Stormy get a head start. Move them forward one.
2. Digger stops to dig a hole. Hotfoot and Stormy move ahead one.
3. Nugget is coming! Move him ahead one.
4. Hotfoot stops to scratch his ear. Move Stormy ahead one.
5. Digger and Nugget dig in. Move them ahead two.
6. Stormy gets nervous. Move ahead one.
7. Hotfoot smells a rabbit. He doesn't move.
8. Nugget sees the finish. Move ahead two.
9. Digger catches up with Stormy.
10. Stormy stops to snap at Digger. Digger rushes ahead two.

Who won? **Digger**

U.S. Facts & Fun • EMC 6305 • ©2005 by Evan-Moor Corp.

Page 87

I KNOW THIS!

Read each sentence.
Fill in the blank with a word or words from the word box.

1. In 1812, we were at war with the **British**
2. The U.S. Army had burned buildings in **Canada**
3. British troops set fire first to the **Capitol** Building.
4. Then they moved toward the **White House**
5. Before they set the fire, they **ate**
6. A **storm** came at midnight.

WORD Box

| Capitol | storm | British |
| Canada | ate | White House |

Page 88

A Few More Facts

Here are more facts about the White House.
Read each clue.
Use the code to tell you what letters to write.

a = 1	e = 5	j = 10	n = 14	r = 18	v = 22
c = 3	h = 8	l = 12	o = 15	s = 19	w = 23
d = 4	i = 9	m = 13	p = 16	t = 20	y = 25

1. He was the first president to live in the White House.

J O H N   A D A M S
10 15 8 14   1 4 1 13 19

2. President Jackson fed some visitors a 1,400-pound block of this.

c h e e s e
3 8 5 5 19 5

3. The president's office is in this wing.

w e s t
23 5 19 20

4. It takes 570 gallons of this to cover the outside of the White House.

p a i n t
16 1 9 14 20

5. This president made the name "White House" official in 1901.

T e d d y
20 5 4 4 25

R o o s e v e l t
18 15 15 19 5 22 5 12 20

Page 89

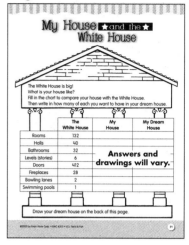

My House ★and the★ White House

The White House is big!
What is your house like?
Fill in the chart to compare your house with the White House.
Then write in how many of each you want to have in your dream house.

	The White House	My House	My Dream House
Rooms	132		
Halls	40		
Bathrooms	32	**Answers and drawings will vary.**	
Levels (stories)	6		
Doors	412		
Fireplaces	28		
Bowling lanes	2		
Swimming pools	1		

Draw your dream house on the back of this page.

Page 91

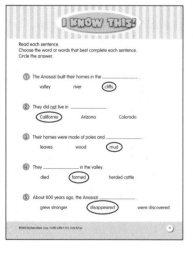

I KNOW THIS!

Read each sentence.
Choose the word or words that best complete each sentence.
Circle the answer.

1. The Anasazi built their homes in the _____
   valley   river   (cliffs)
2. They did not live in _____
   (California)   Arizona   Colorado
3. Their homes were made of poles and _____
   leaves   wood   (mud)
4. They _____ in the valley.
   died   (farmed)   herded cattle
5. About 800 years ago, the Anasazi _____
   grew stronger   (disappeared)   were discovered

Page 92

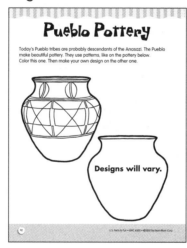

Pueblo Pottery

Today's Pueblo tribes are probably descendants of the Anasazi. The Pueblo make beautiful pottery. They use patterns, like on the pottery below. Color this one. Then make your own design on the other one.

Designs will vary.

Page 93

Triangle Maze

Triangles and circles were common designs of the Pueblo.
Follow the maze to find out which gateway leads to the Anasazi sun in the middle.

Page 95

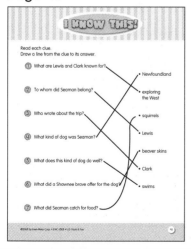

I KNOW THIS!

Read each clue.
Draw a line from the clue to its answer.

1. What are Lewis and Clark known for?
2. To whom did Seaman belong?
3. Who wrote about the trip?
4. What kind of dog was Seaman?
5. What does this kind of dog do well?
6. What did a Shawnee brave offer for the dog?
7. What did Seaman catch for food?

- Newfoundland
- exploring the West
- squirrels
- Lewis
- beaver skins
- Clark
- swims

Page 96

Dog Facts

Unscramble the word to finish each dog fact.

1. Dogs only sweat from the bottoms of their **tefe**. **feet**
2. Dalmatians are born all **tihwe**. No spots! **white**
3. Newfoundlands have webbed feet to help them **msiw**. **swim**
4. Don't **mesil** at a strange dog. It might think you are showing your teeth to start a fight! **smile**
5. A greyhound can **nru** up to 42 mph. **run**
6. All puppies are born **dlinb** and deaf. They will begin to see and hear at about two weeks old. **blind**

Page 97

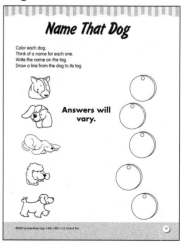

Name That Dog

Color each dog.
Think of a name for each one.
Write the name on the tag.
Draw a line from the dog to its tag.

Answers will vary.

Page 99

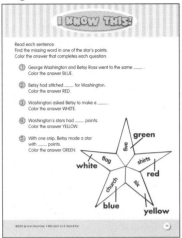

I KNOW THIS!

Read each sentence.
Find the missing word in one of the star's points.
Color the answer that completes each question.

1. George Washington and Betsy Ross went to the same _____.
   Color the answer BLUE.
2. Betsy had stitched _____ for Washington.
   Color the answer RED.
3. Washington asked Betsy to make a _____.
   Color the answer WHITE.
4. Washington's stars had _____ points.
   Color the answer YELLOW.
5. With one snip, Betsy made a star with _____ points.
   Color the answer GREEN.

Page 100

Make a Star

You can make a star just like Betsy Ross did. Have an adult help you.
Follow these steps:

1. Start with a half sheet of copier paper. Fold in half and label corners A, B, C, D as shown.
2. Locate the center of edge labeled A–B and mark with pencil. Fold C to this point.
3. Fold flap A down as shown.
4. Fold bottom right up to meet top left edge.
5. Rotate shape upward to look like an ice-cream cone. Mark 14 cm from bottom point on the left side. Mark 3.3 cm from bottom point on the right side. Draw a line between these points. Cut on the line.
6. Unfold the small piece that was cut away. This is the star.

Page 101

Red, White, & Blue
Clues

Color the R areas red.
Color the B areas blue.
Leave the W areas white.

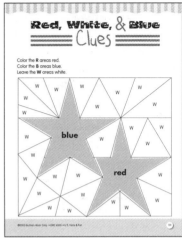

Page 103

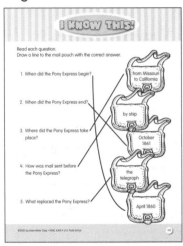

I KNOW THIS!

Read each question.
Draw a line to the mail pouch with the correct answer.

1. When did the Pony Express begin?
2. When did the Pony Express end?
3. Where did the Pony Express take place?
4. How was mail sent before the Pony Express?
5. What replaced the Pony Express?

- from Missouri to California
- by ship
- October 1861
- the telegraph
- April 1860

Page 104

MAIL CALL!

Here are more Pony Express facts!
Unscramble the bold words.
Write the words on the envelopes.

1. The Pony Express ran night and **yda**. — day
2. A Pony Express **dreir** made $100 a month. — rider
3. Each rider rode about 60 **lsmie**. — miles
4. A horse ran about 10 miles per **uorh**. — hour
5. About 400 **srsohe** were used. — horses
6. A rider had to weigh **sels** than 125 pounds. — less

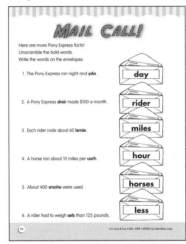

Page 105

PONY EXPRESS MAP

Follow the Pony Express through eight states.
Color each state. Then number them in "route" order, east to west.

7. Nevada - green stripes
6. Utah - red dots
3. Nebraska - red stripes
1. Missouri - blue stripes
2. Kansas - orange dots
8. California - blue dots
4. Colorado - green dots
5. Wyoming - orange stripes

Color according to color key.

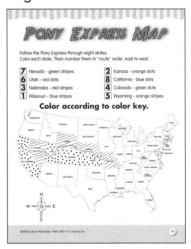

Page 107

I KNOW THIS!

Read each sentence.
Fill in the bull's-eye if it is true.
Mark an X on the outside ring if it is false.

	HIT	MISS
1. Little Annie Oakley was poor.		
2. She never left her family.		
3. Annie helped her family.		
4. She planted a garden for food.		
5. Annie sang to earn money.		
6. She was a better shot than most men.		
7. Her nickname was "Girl with a Gun."		

Page 108

A GIRL AND HER GUN

Annie has to practice shooting.
Can you help her?
Get Annie through the maze from her house to the target area.

Page 109

A Really TRICKY SHOT

Annie was known for her trick shooting.
Find the answer to each problem.
Then connect the answers in order in the picture to show how Annie's bullet traveled.

1. $4 + 4 + 4 - 6 + 2 =$ **8**
2. $10 - 5 - 4 + 7 - 3 =$ **5**
3. $1 + 2 + 3 + 4 + 5 + 6 =$ **21**
4. $10 + 10 + 10 + 10 - 20 - 8 + 7 =$ **19**
5. $12 - 7 + 6 + 3 - 5 =$ **9**

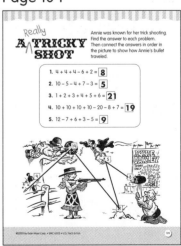

Page 111

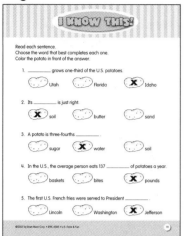

I KNOW THIS!

Read each sentence.
Choose the word that best completes each one.
Color the potato in front of the answer.

1. _____ grows one-third of the U.S. potatoes.
   ◯ Utah   ◯ Florida   ✖ Idaho

2. Its _____ is just right.
   ✖ soil   ◯ butter   ◯ sand

3. A potato is three-fourths _____ .
   ◯ sugar   ✖ water   ◯ soil

4. In the U.S., the average person eats 137 _____ of potatoes a year.
   ◯ baskets   ◯ bites   ✖ pounds

5. The first U.S. French fries were served to President _____ .
   ◯ Lincoln   ◯ Washington   ✖ Jefferson

Page 112

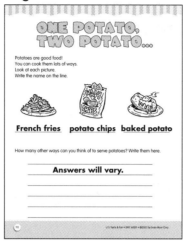

ONE POTATO, TWO POTATO...

Potatoes are good food!
You can cook them lots of ways.
Look at each picture.
Write the name on the line.

French fries   **potato chips**   **baked potato**

How many other ways can you think of to serve potatoes? Write them here.

Answers will vary.

Page 113

POTATO JOKES

Read each joke.
Color the funny pictures.

Q: How does a potato say good-bye?
A: "Later, tater!"

Q: What does Santa Tater say?
A: Ida-ho-ho-ho!

Q: What do you call a potato at the ice rink?
A: A tater skater!

Q: What do you call a bad potato?
A: A spud dud!

Q: Why couldn't the little potato spell "Mississippi"?
A: Because he didn't have enough i's!

Page 115

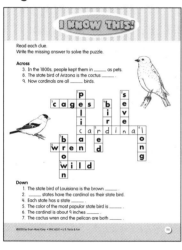

I KNOW THIS!

Read each clue.
Write the missing answer to solve the puzzle.

Across
3. In the 1800s, people kept them in _____ as pets.
8. The state bird of Arizona is the cactus _____ .
9. Now cardinals are all _____ birds.

Crossword answers:
cages, birds, seven, cardinal, song, blue, wren, red, brown, wild

Down
1. The state bird of Louisiana is the brown _____ .
2. _____ states have the cardinal as their state bird.
4. Each state has a state _____ .
5. The color of the most popular state bird is _____ .
6. The cardinal is about 9 inches _____ .
7. The cactus wren and the pelican are both _____ .

Page 116

Beautiful Birds

Each of these is a state bird.
Can you find pictures of them in a book?
Color them as they actually look.

1. Maryland — orange & black — Baltimore Oriole
2. Connecticut, Michigan, Wisconsin — brown & red — American Robin
3. Missouri, New York — blue — Eastern Bluebird
4. Iowa, New Jersey — yellow & black — American Goldfinch
5. Ohio, Indiana, Illinois, Kentucky, Virginia, West Virginia, North Carolina — red — Northern Cardinal
6. Maine, Massachusetts — light gray & black — Black-Capped Chickadee

What is your state bird? **Answers will vary.**

Page 117

Funny Feathered Friends

Read each riddle.
Find the answer below.
Write the correct bird on the line.

1. Which old bird is a good outfielder?   **gray flycatcher**
2. Which bird is always sad?   **bluebird**
3. Which bird always steals?   **robin**
4. Which bird joined the marathon?   **roadrunner**
5. Which bird didn't know the words to the songs?   **hummingbird**
6. Which bird is always out of breath?   **puffin**
7. Which bird eats big buildings?   **barn swallow**

WORD Box → roadrunner puffin gray flycatcher bluebird hummingbird robin barn swallow

Page 119

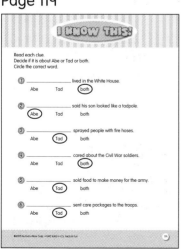

I KNOW THIS!

Read each clue.
Decide if it is about Abe or Tad or both.
Circle the correct word.

1. _____ lived in the White House.
   Abe   Tad   (both)

2. _____ said his son looked like a tadpole.
   (Abe)   Tad   both

3. _____ sprayed people with fire hoses.
   Abe   (Tad)   both

4. _____ cared about the Civil War soldiers.
   Abe   Tad   (both)

5. _____ sold food to make money for the army.
   Abe   (Tad)   both

6. _____ sent care packages to the troops.
   Abe   (Tad)   both

Page 120

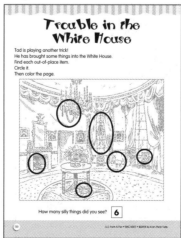

Trouble in the White House

Tad is playing another trick!
He has brought some things into the White House.
Find each out-of-place item.
Circle it.
Then color the page.

How many silly things did you see? **6**

Page 121

Three-Letter Words

Read each clue.
Write the three-letter answer.
Finish each square.

1 across - Thomas's nickname
2 down - a small circle
3 across - a cat or dog is one
1 down - not the bottom

Grid: T a d / o o / p e t

4 across - Tad had a lot of this
5 down - you take one when tired
6 across - to tear something
4 down - not against

Grid: f u n / o a / r i p

7 across - Tad's dad
8 down - can be fried or scrambled
9 across - young Abe cut this
7 down - everything

Grid: A b e / l g / l o g

10 across - father
11 down - to make a hole
12 across - a funny trick
10 down - grown-up puppy

Grid: d a d / o i / g a g

Page 123

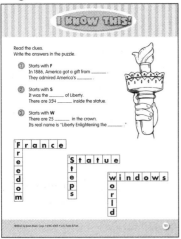

I KNOW THIS!

Read the clues.
Write the answers in the puzzle.

1. Starts with **F**
In 1886, America got a gift from ____ .
They admired America's ____ .

2. Starts with **S**
It was the ____ of Liberty.
There are 354 ____ inside the statue.

3. Starts with **W**
There are 25 ____ in the crown.
Its real name is "Liberty Enlightening the ____ ."

Puzzle answers: France, Freedom, Statue, Steps, windows, world

Page 124

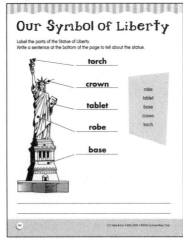

Our Symbol of Liberty

Label the parts of the Statue of Liberty.
Write a sentence at the bottom of the page to tell about the statue.

torch
crown
tablet
robe
base

robe
tablet
base
crown
torch

Page 125

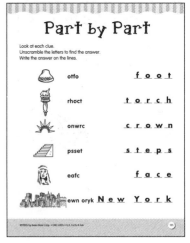

Part by Part

Look at each clue.
Unscramble the letters to find the answer.
Write the answer on the lines.

otfo	f o o t
rhoct	t o r c h
onwrc	c r o w n
psset	s t e p s
eafc	f a c e
ewn oryk	N e w Y o r k

Page 127

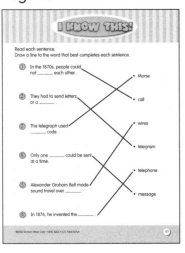

I KNOW THIS!

Read each sentence.
Draw a line to the word that best completes each sentence.

1. In the 1870s, people could not ____ each other. — Morse
2. They had to send letters or a ____ . — call
3. The telegraph used ____ code. — wires
4. Only one ____ could be sent at a time. — telegram
5. Alexander Graham Bell made sound travel over ____ . — telephone
6. In 1876, he invented the ____ . — message

Page 128

Find the Phones

Find the eight phones in this picture.
Color each one.

Page 129

Mr. Watson, Come Here!

The first words spoken over a telephone were, "Mr. Watson—come here—I want to see you."
Alexander Graham Bell was "calling" his assistant, Thomas Watson.

Help Mr. Bell's message get to Mr. Watson.

Mr. Watson ...

Page 131

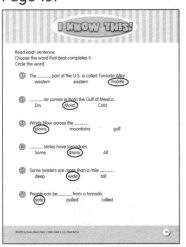

I KNOW THIS!

Read each sentence.
Choose the word that best completes it.
Circle the word.

1. The ____ part of the U.S. is called Tornado Alley.
western   eastern   (middle)

2. ____ air comes in from the Gulf of Mexico.
Dry   (Moist)   Cold

3. Winds blow across the ____ .
(plains)   mountains   gulf

4. ____ states have tornadoes.
Some   (Many)   All

5. Some twisters are more than a mile ____ .
deep   (wide)   tall

6. People can be ____ from a tornado.
(safe)   pulled   called

Page 132

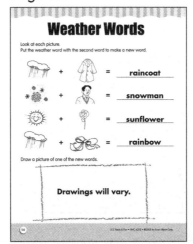

Weather Words

Look at each picture.
Put the weather word with the second word to make a new word.

____ + ____ = **raincoat**
____ + ____ = **snowman**
____ + ____ = **sunflower**
____ + ____ = **rainbow**

Draw a picture of one of the new words.

Drawings will vary.

Page 133

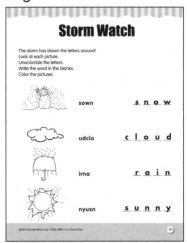

Storm Watch

The storm has blown the letters around!
Look at each picture.
Unscramble the letters.
Write the word in the blanks.
Color the pictures.

sown	s n o w
udclo	c l o u d
irna	r a i n
nyusn	s u n n y

Page 135

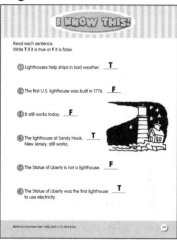

I KNOW THIS!

Read each sentence.
Write **T** if it is true or **F** if is false.

1. Lighthouses help ships in bad weather. **T**

2. The first U.S. lighthouse was built in 1776. **F**

3. It still works today. **F**

4. The lighthouse at Sandy Hook, New Jersey, still works. **T**

5. The Statue of Liberty is not a lighthouse. **F**

6. The Statue of Liberty was the first lighthouse to use electricity. **T**

Page 136

Connect the Dots

Connect the dots from **1** to **27**.
Color the picture you uncover.

Page 137

Name That Lighthouse

Look at each picture clue below.
Find the name of the lighthouse.
Draw a line to the name.

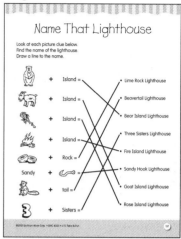

Page 139

I KNOW THIS!

Read the clues.
Write the answers in the puzzle.

1. Starts with **F**
   These fall over the falls.
   Niagara _____ is the second-largest area of waterfalls in the world.

2. Starts with **W**
   More than 750,000 gallons of _____ go over the falls each second.
   Niagara Falls is made up of two _____.

3. Starts with **S**
   They "go with the flow" and _____ along.
   Some fish end up in the United _____.

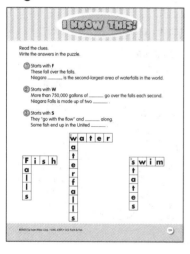

Page 140

LET'S GO FISHING!

Many kinds of fish swim in the Niagara River between Lake Erie and Lake Ontario.
Find the fish in the word search below.
Circle each one.

WORD Box ▶▶▶ bass carp pike perch trout salmon walleye muskie

Page 141

FISHY FUN

These fish are going over the Falls!
Find the one that is different. Circle it.

Page 143

I KNOW THIS!

Read each sentence.
Color the bell beside the answer that best completes each sentence.

1. The Liberty Bell broke _____ times.
   2 **3** (X) 5

2. The bell was first made in _____.
   Philadelphia New York **England** (X)

3. It was a mix of copper and _____.
   tin (X) iron silver

4. The last time it broke was during a _____.
   funeral (X) parade battle

5. You can see the Liberty Bell in _____.
   Washington, D.C. New York **Philadelphia** (X)

Page 144

Cracked Picture

This picture is cracked up!
Something is hidden in it.
To find it, color the areas as follows:

B = blue **E** = red **L** = yellow

Color according to directions.

yellow

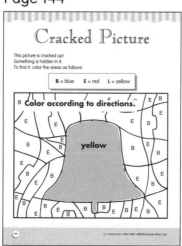

Page 145

You Crack Me Up!

Read each riddle.
Draw a line to the best ending.

1. When should you ring the Liberty Bell?

2. What did the people eat when they rang the Liberty Bell?

3. Why didn't the Liberty Bell ask the Blue Bell to marry him?

4. What happens when you tell the Liberty Bell a joke?

- He didn't have a very good "ring."
- Crackers!
- It cracks up!
- At the "crack" of dawn.

Page 147

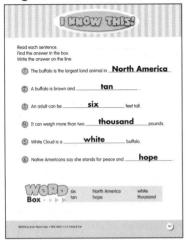

I KNOW THIS!

Read each sentence.
Find the answer in the box.
Write the answer on the line.

1. The buffalo is the largest land animal in **North America**.

2. A buffalo is brown and **tan**.

3. An adult can be **six** feet tall.

4. It can weigh more than two **thousand** pounds.

5. White Cloud is a **white** buffalo.

6. Native Americans say she stands for peace and **hope**.

WORD Box

six	North America	white
tan	hope	thousand

Page 148

Missing Buffalo

Help the albino buffalo find his herd.

Page 149

Buffalo Match-Up

Look at each picture.
Label each one.
Use the word box for help.
Then color each picture.

buffalo nickel	Buffalo Bill	Buffalo, New York
buffalo grass	buffalo wings	water buffalo

WORD Box

buffalo wings	buffalo grass	buffalo nickel
Buffalo Bill	water buffalo	Buffalo, NY

Page 151

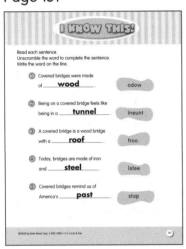

I KNOW THIS!

Read each sentence.
Unscramble the word to complete the sentence.
Write the word on the line.

1. Covered bridges were made of **wood** — odow

2. Being on a covered bridge feels like being in a **tunnel** — lneunt

3. A covered bridge is a wood bridge with a **roof** — froo

4. Today, bridges are made of iron and **steel** — lstee

5. Covered bridges remind us of America's **past** — stap

Page 152

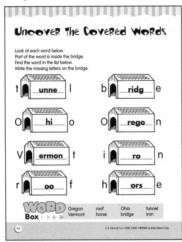

Uncover the Covered Words

Look at each word below.
Part of the word is inside the bridge.
Find the word in the list below.
Write the missing letters on the bridge.

t **unne** l

b **ridg** e

O **hi** o

O **rego** n

V **ermon** t

i **ro** n

r **oo** f

h **ors** e

WORD Box

Oregon	roof	Ohio	tunnel
Vermont	horse	bridge	iron

Page 153

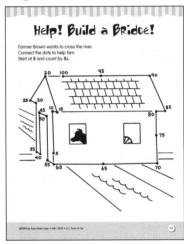

Help! Build a Bridge!

Farmer Brown wants to cross the river.
Connect the dots to help him.
Start at 5 and count by 5s.

Page 155

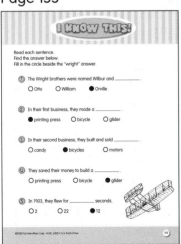

I KNOW THIS!

Read each sentence.
Find the answer below.
Fill in the circle beside the "wright" answer.

1. The Wright brothers were named Wilbur and _____
   ○ Otto ○ William ● Orville

2. In their first business, they made a _____
   ● printing press ○ bicycle ○ glider

3. In their second business, they built and sold _____
   ○ candy ● bicycles ○ motors

4. They saved their money to build a _____
   ○ printing press ○ bicycle ● glider

5. In 1903, they flew for _____ seconds.
   ○ 2 ○ 22 ● 12

Page 156

Just Alike

Find the two airplanes that are alike.
Color both of them the same.

Page 157

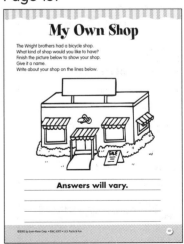

My Own Shop

The Wright brothers had a bicycle shop.
What kind of shop would you like to have?
Finish the picture below to show your shop.
Give it a name.
Write about your shop on the lines below.

Answers will vary.

Page 159

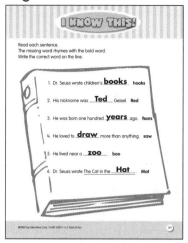

I KNOW THIS!

Read each sentence.
The missing word rhymes with the bold word.
Write the correct word on the line.

1. Dr. Seuss wrote children's **books**. hooks
2. His nickname was **Ted** Geisel. Red
3. He was born one hundred **years** ago. fears
4. He loved to **draw** more than anything. saw
5. He lived near a **zoo**. boo
6. Dr. Seuss wrote The Cat in the **Hat**. Mat

Page 160

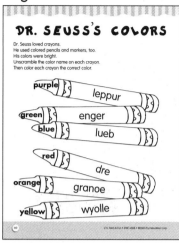

DR. SEUSS'S COLORS

Dr. Seuss loved crayons.
He used colored pencils and markers, too.
His colors were bright.
Unscramble the color name on each crayon.
Then color each crayon the correct color.

- purple — leppur
- green — enger
- blue — lueb
- red — dre
- orange — granoe
- yellow — wyolle

Page 161

ON A BOAT? WITH A GOAT?

Fill in the blank with a word that rhymes with the bold word.
Use the picture clues.

1. I see a **sled**. It is under my __bed__
2. Go get that **dog**! He's chasing a __frog__
3. See that **cat**! It's sitting on my __hat__
4. We have a **pig**. It wears a __wig__
5. Look in my **mug**! I think it's a __bug__

Page 163

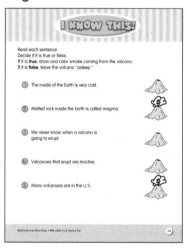

I KNOW THIS!

Read each sentence.
Decide if it is true or false.
If it is **true**, draw and color smoke coming from the volcano.
If it is **false**, leave the volcano "asleep."

1. The inside of the Earth is very cold.
2. Melted rock inside the Earth is called magma.
3. We never know when a volcano is going to erupt.
4. Volcanoes that erupt are inactive.
5. Many volcanoes are in the U.S.

Page 164

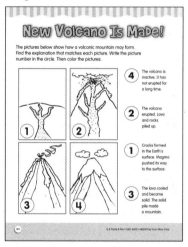

New Volcano Is Made!

The pictures below show how a volcanic mountain may form.
Find the explanation that matches each picture. Write the picture number in the circle. Then color the pictures.

4. The volcano is inactive. It has not erupted for a long time.

2. The volcano erupted. Lava and rocks piled up.

1. Cracks formed in the Earth's surface. Magma pushed its way to the surface.

3. The lava cooled and became solid. The solid pile made a mountain.

Page 165

Red-Hot Puzzle

Read each clue.
Write the answer in the puzzle.

Puzzle answers: volcano, inside, melts, magma, Hawaii, lava

Across
3. Inside the Earth, rock is so hot that it _____.
5. Hot _____ may come out of a volcano.

Down
1. When pressure builds up, a _____ erupts.
2. The _____ of the Earth is very hot.
3. Hot rock inside the Earth is called _____.
4. Volcanoes can be found in _____, Alaska, and the western U.S.

Page 167

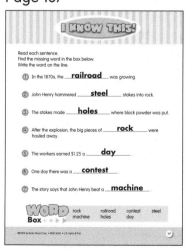

I KNOW THIS!

Read each sentence.
Find the missing word in the box below.
Write the word on the line.

1. In the 1870s, the __railroad__ was growing.
2. John Henry hammered __steel__ stakes into rock.
3. The stakes made __holes__ where black powder was put.
4. After the explosion, the big pieces of __rock__ were hauled away.
5. The workers earned $1.25 a __day__.
6. One day there was a __contest__.
7. The story says that John Henry beat a __machine__.

WORD Box rock railroad contest steel machine holes day

Page 168

BUILDING THE RAILROAD

Follow the maze to get to the next town.
Watch out for the big rocks!

Answers may vary.

Page 169

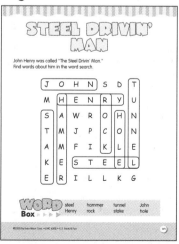

STEEL DRIVIN' MAN

John Henry was called "The Steel Drivin' Man."
Find words about him in the word search.

WORD Box steel hammer tunnel John Henry rock stake hole

Page 171

I KNOW THIS!

Read the clues.
Write one letter on each line.
The letters in the boxes will spell another word from the story.

1. The caves are like deep, dark _____
2. Mammoth has the biggest bunch of _____ in the world.
3. They are _____ to many odd animals.
4. The caves go on for 335 _____
5. The cave spiders have no _____
6. Mammoth Cave National Park is in _____
7. There is almost no _____ in the caves.

	m	a	z	e	s
c	a	v	e	s	
h	o	m	e		
	m	i	l	e	s
	c	o	l	o	r
K	e	n	t	u	c	k	y
l	i	g	h	t	

The word is the boxes is **mammoth**

It means **big**   dark   maze   big

Page 172

Hidden Animals

Mammoth Cave is home to many animals.
Unscramble the animal names below.
Find the animals in the cave and color them.

orgf **frog**   tab **bat**   tra **rat**
hifs **fish**   prised **spider**   tickerc **cricket**

Page 173

Cave Maze

Find your way through the cave maze.

Page 175

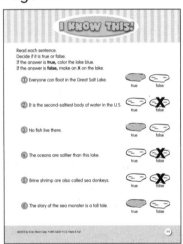

I KNOW THIS!

Read each sentence.
Decide if it is true or false.
If the answer is **true**, color the lake blue.
If the answer is **false**, make an **X** on the lake.

1. Everyone can float in the Great Salt Lake.   true / false
2. It is the second-saltiest body of water in the U.S.   true / **X** false
3. No fish live there.   true / false
4. The oceans are saltier than this lake.   true / **X** false
5. Brine shrimp are also called sea donkeys.   true / **X** false
6. The story of the sea monster is a tall tale.   true / false

Page 176

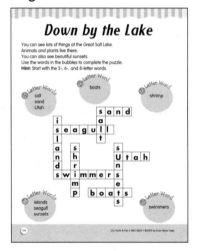

Down by the Lake

You can see lots of things at the Great Salt Lake.
Animals and plants live there.
You can also **see** beautiful sunsets.
Use the words in the bubbles to complete the puzzle.
Hint: Start with the 5-, 6-, and 8-letter words.

3 Letter Word: salt, sand, Utah
5 Letter Word: boats
6 Letter Word: shrimp
8 Letter Words: islands, seagull, sunsets
7 Letter Word: swimmers

(crossword puzzle: sand, salt, island, seagull, shrimp, Utah, swimmers, boats, sunsets)

Page 177

Salty or Sweet?

Look at all this food!
Color the things that taste salty **yellow**.
Color the things that taste sweet **blue**.

yellow   blue   blue
blue   blue
blue   yellow
yellow   yellow   blue